The Preacher

and

His Preaching

by
Dr. J. D. O'Donnell

Randall House Publications
114 Bush Road—P. O. Box 17306
Nashville, TN 37217
First Edition 1974
Second Edition 2000

CONTENTS

PREFACE

This book is not being written to supersede or substitute for the great classics in the field of homiletics. The works of Broadus, Pattison, and others have made a contribution to the work of the ministry that can never be measured. The purpose of this book is to meet a specific need.

As the author has ministered in various parts of the country, he has become aware of many young preachers who need a book to read dealing with the first principles of sermon building and preaching. It is for this reason that he takes pen in hand to write this book. It is hoped that this book will be helpful especially to beginning college students and to preachers who will never have the privilege of sitting in the classroom.

God needs every man who will answer His call. But the need is for every man who answers the call to develop every talent which he has to its greatest potential. May this book serve as a challenge to each reader to spur him to become one of God's most useful servants.

– Dr. J. D. O'Donnell

INTRODUCTION

The Apostle Paul admonished Timothy, his son in the ministry, to "preach the word." To Titus, another son, he said, "But speak thou the things which become sound doctrine." A part of Paul's final thrust, as revealed in his pastoral letters to Timothy and Titus, was to prepare these younger men for active preaching ministries.

Every true minister prays that God will use his life and preaching to call forth young men into the ministry of proclaiming the gospel. However, most ministers do not nurture youthful preachers as they should. There may be a public announcement of the call and a spasmodic opportunity to preach but that is where the fatherly pastoral concern all too often ends.

It is to correct this fault that Dr. J. D. O'Donnell has written this brief, but succinct and helpful, book for beginning preachers. This could well be the first book which the pastor would place in the hand of each young preacher in his flock. This book could serve as the basis for periods of pastoral teaching and guidance. I believe that my own ministry, especially during my teenage years, would have been more effective and fruitful if I could have been introduced to such a helpful guide.

Dr. O'Donnell has worthy credentials for preparing this book. His life has touched literally hundreds of young preachers in his ministry of more than a quarter of a century. As Professor of Bible and Homiletics in one college and later as President of another college, he was in almost daily contact with men in training for the ministry of preaching. And besides this, Dr. O'Donnell loves preaching and he loves fellow-preachers.

I am personally grateful for this book. I am certain it is sent forth with the prayer for God to call *more* ministers and that these become *better prepared* ministers.

Charles A. Thigpen

1
The Preacher

To be called a pastor is great. To be called a minister is fine. But to be called a *preacher* should chill the spine of any God-called man. It is a matter of pride to be so honored, but it is a matter of humility as one recognizes the enormous responsibility of being a preacher, a spokesman for God. The Greek word for preacher refers to a herald, a messenger, or a proclaimer (1 Timothy 2:7; 2 Timothy 1:11). A more specific word is used in the New Testament which refers to one who announces glad tidings or who preaches the gospel (translated *evangelist* in Acts 21:8; Ephesians 4:11; 2 Timothy 4:5). Either is a spokesman for God in Christian usage.

A. Marks of a True Preacher

When a man calls himself a preacher, people generally respond with respect. That respect is due only to certain ones, however. It is due to those who bear the marks of a true preacher.

1. A true preacher is marked by utter dedication.

Just as Paul could say, "This one thing I do," so the preacher should be totally sold out to his ministry. Like Moody who at one time sold shoes to make a living, his main task will remain preaching. Francis of Assissi once said, "Unless you preach everywhere you go, there is no use to go anywhere to preach."

2. *A true preacher is marked by great humility of heart.* This is derived from his recognition of three things: (1) the magnitude of his task; (2) his own unworthiness; and (3) that whatever his work may seem to achieve, it is God's doing and not his own.

3. *A true preacher is a man of authority.* Though a bondslave of Christ he has an appointment as His herald and His ambassador. As to Paul so He has said to the preacher of today that He will "make thee a minister" (Acts 26:16). The preacher's authority is based upon three factors: (1) It is God's Word which we are to deliver. (2) The testimony of the church supports him. (3) He has come into possession of the Word in his personal experience and is now possessed by it. Like Jeremiah that Word appears as "a burning fire shut up in my bones" (Jeremiah 20:9). Always with a growing vision, the true preacher is a man of fire.

B. QUALIFICATIONS OF A PREACHER

Some groups ordain every man who announces a call whether he gives evidences of a genuine call from God or not. This should not be true. God's man will

8

meet certain high qualifications among which are the following.

1. He must be born again and especially called of God. Evidences of a changed life resulting from a spiritual rebirth should precede his call from God. A call from God arises from two things. The first is the personal nature of God. He is a Person who reveals himself to His creatures. He chooses other persons to be His heralds or ambassadors to proclaim His Word. The second thing out of which a call arises is the sovereignty of God. As the Ruler of the universe, it is only natural to suppose that He will choose and appoint men for the specific task of mediating His message to others.

2. He must love Jesus and lost souls. The message of the New Testament Church spread like a wild fire. They were in love with Jesus who had given himself to save lost souls. Thrilled by that message, they "went every where preaching the word" (Acts 8:4). The need of the world is for a new generation of preachers so enraptured by Jesus and burdened for lost souls.

3. He must be a student of the Scriptures. A deacon who enjoyed leading young ministers into a study of the Scriptures said one day of a young man who had announced a call, "He will never make a preacher. He won't study his Bible." The years to come proved him correct. That man did not make a preacher. It is the Word of God which we are to herald. We must be full of that Word.

4. He must be a man of prayer. All of God's spokesmen through the centuries have been men of communion with God. Abraham, Samuel, Jeremiah, Daniel, all were well-acquainted with God in prayer. Our main memory of Elijah was that "he prayed" (James 5:17). Let us remember too that our Lord was a man of constant prayer.

5. *He must be morally clean.* "Blameless" was Paul's term for a preacher (1 Timothy 3:2). "Keep thyself pure" was his admonition to a young preacher (1 Timothy 5:22). Your preaching will be what you are. Habits, attitudes, convictions, and experiences will flavor your message. Peculiar temptations will come to a young minister as they did to Joseph. For this reason he should "take heed unto thyself" (1 Timothy 4:16).

6. *He must be fit for his work spiritually, physically, mentally, and educationally.* Spiritual preparation can come through constant communion with God through prayer and a study of the Word of God. The Word of God should never be just what you preach. It should ever be the source of the preacher's spiritual food as well.

Timothy was urged to "study" (2 Timothy 2:15). He was also urged to "give attendance to reading" (1 Timothy 4:13). Communion through books with the great minds of the centuries is a means of continued education. Like a boxer or some other athlete, the preacher is never out of training for his task. To keep mentally alert, he must read and study.

The body is not to be neglected. Though Paul wrote that "bodily exercise profiteth little," we must admit that it does profit some. An overweight, lazy man

10

will not give a good impression as a preacher. Obesity in a preacher is unbecoming to his position and calling.

C. ELEMENTS IN A CALL TO PREACH

Though the exact call of an individual cannot be described, the experience of many preachers indicate several common elements. Some like Paul receive their call through a crisis experience, but more generally the following elements are involved.

1. An abiding conviction aroused by the inward urge of the Holy Spirit. A conviction begins which cannot be lost. This author has advised young men sensing a call, "Don't preach if you don't have to." One divinely called cannot easily escape the conviction. A truly called man will not easily suppress the promptings of the Holy Spirit.

2. A compassionate heart for sinners. Richard Baxter advised young men to "preach as a dying man to dying men." This is what it is all about. No other issue is so vital to the preacher as saving souls. A called man must sense this lostness of man.

3. The divine ordering of God's providences. The call of most men has been deepened by the sense of need around then. Benjamin Randall was struck in the soul upon learning of George Whitefield's death. He must have sensed that a gap would be left by this man's death. A scarcity of preachers often serves as a burden upon some men to make them answer God's call.

11

4. Some deep impression from the Word of God which increases the abiding conviction. In the author's own experience it was Jeremiah's woe upon his nation because of their evil shepherds that deepened the burden for preaching (Jeremiah 50:6). Just as the Word of God brings conviction for sin, so it contains God's commandment to go. Reading of the Word cannot but intensify the call of any man.

D. REASONS FOR PREACHING

Why should a man devote his time, his life, to a ministry of preaching? When he answers the call, he should have reasons for doing so.

1. It is the divine plan to spread the gospel. Paul said that "it pleased God by the foolishness of preaching to save them that believe" (1 Corinthians 1:21). No new method has ever arisen to displace preaching. In fact, every revival of religion has been marked by a revival of God's plan to spread the gospel—preaching.

2. It is the means of bringing faith and regeneration to hearers of the Word. As "ambassadors for Christ" we have the ministry of reconciling alien sinners to God (2 Corinthians 5:20). "How shall they hear without a preacher?" (Romans 10:14) is a probing question. Before men "call" and "believe," the preacher must preach.

3. It is the means by which believers are edified. Paul described the preached word as that "which

12

effectually worketh also in you that believe" (1 Thessalonians 2:13). The Word of God is "profitable for doctrine, for reproof, for correction, for instruction in righteousness" (2 Timothy 3:16).

E. THE NATURE OF THE PREACHER'S TASK

The task of the preacher has various elements in it. Some have summed up its nature as being pastoral, promotional, and prophetical. Probably the three most basic elements of that task can be summed up in the following terms.

1. Mediatorial. Though the church has no priestly system because every man can have direct access to God, yet there is a need for mediating between God and man. The preacher is to be a soul winner. Andrew brought Peter (John 1:41). Philip brought Nathanael (John 1:46). So the pattern goes. The preacher as a man of God will always be presenting God to man and interceding to God for man.

2. Pastoral. As a pastor the duties of a preacher will be varied. He will be seeking to feed the flock, administer the affairs of the church, and be a builder of the work in general. He must be careful lest he get bogged down in administration and promotion and forget his main task.

3. Prophetical. A prophet is a spokesman for God. He "forth tells" to people the message of God. His main task is preaching. Not to be forgotten is the element of

13

"foretelling" also in his ministry. In the line of prophets of old he continues to tell of things that shall be—death, judgment, Heaven, Hell.

This age is characterized by the unreal in preaching. Men with somber "ministerial" tones fill many pulpits giving book reviews and talking on social issues. As one man told this writer, "I can read that in the newspaper." To these that are missing the real nature of the task, the world cries, "Physician, heal thyself." The true preacher from God needs to be marked by that which is real and not by the artificial. He needs to be *real in his devotion to God.* The world hates the counterfeit. They see through an actor. They detect and detest hypocrisy. The preacher must be *real in his language.* Superfluous high sounding language should never characterize a preacher. The early apostles came "not in excellency of speech." The true preacher must be *real in his total attitude toward his message.* Those New Testament preachers were swept off their feet because of the glory of their revelation. Lost man now had a Savior. Thrilled by that message they went out to tell lost men the good news. Could one of them come back today, he would ask, "What has happened?"

A preacher to have a vital ministry must never grow lax. James Steward said, "We have no right in our preaching to waste time on side-issues and irrelevancies." We are to "preach Christ." To preach Christ in the New Testament had two points: Christ died. Christ arose. This was the vitality of their message.

14

To keep a vital message, do these things: (1) Aim at results. (2) Expect mighty things to happen. (3) Realize that every soul is of an infinite value. (4) Never forget that Christ is with you in your preaching and your work.

2

Preaching and Homiletics

What is preaching? If one is to be a preacher, he
should ever be a student of the art of preaching. The art
of preaching is referred to as homiletics.

A. THE MEANING OF PREACHING

The meaning of preaching has been described in
various ways. As already mentioned, the Greek word
means to herald or proclaim. In particular, the Christian
community coined a word which means to proclaim the
good news. The good news (gospel) was the saving
message which resulted from the death of Christ for
man's sin and His resurrection for our justification. A
more formal definition of preaching has been given as
"the communication of divine truth through personality
with persuasion by one divinely called, for God's glory
and man's good."

Three basic elements stand out in that definition:
(1) the Sender, who is God; (2) the sent one, who is the
preacher; and (3) a communication, which is the Word

16

of God. These elements must always be present when there is preaching. The Sender must be involved for Paul said, "And how shall they preach, except they be sent?" (Romans 10:15). It is because of who the Sender is that Paul cried out saying, "Necessity is laid upon me; yea, woe is unto me, if I preach not the gospel!" (1 Corinthians 9:16). Because God is the Sender, a solemn obligation is laid upon the preacher.

The preacher is the one sent. One of the earliest terms to describe New Testament preachers is *apostle.* This word refers to a "sent forth one." The followers of Jesus were at first disciples (students, or learners). But after the initial training period they became apostles (sent forth ones). One of Paul's questions was, "How shall they hear without a preacher?" (Romans 10:14). The answer is that they will not hear since it is God's plan to save the world through preaching.

The other element is divine truth or God's Word. The prophetic blessing is upon those who preach the Word. Isaiah wrote: "How beautiful are the feet of them that preach the gospel of peace, and bring glad tidings of good things" (Romans 10:15). The preacher has no message if he does not preach the Word. Every message, every admonition, and every exhortation must be based upon the Scriptures. Every persuasion directed toward the congregation must be supported by the Bible.

Every preacher should always be aware that he is not producing an essay or just a speech. He is attempting to communicate the divine truth which God has revealed in the Scriptures. Through words carefully chosen through prayer he must communicate a Person to his hearers. That Person is Jesus Christ.

B. THE PLACE OF PREACHING

Since preaching is to make men God-conscious and to translate His message to men, its place in Christianity needs to be defined.

1. Preaching is characteristic of Christianity. Christianity was announced by John the Baptist who came "preaching in the wilderness" (Matthew 3:1). From that day to this preaching has dominated all other means of spreading the gospel. The printed page has been used as well as many other means of spreading the Word, but preaching ever remains *the* means of telling the good news.

It is interesting to note that no other religion has ever made preaching such a vital part of its worship. This is also true of most of the religious sects. The "foolishness of preaching" bears no appeal to the natural man.

2. Preaching was prominent in the ministry of Jesus. Shortly after the temptation in the wilderness, it is reported by Matthew that "Jesus began to preach" (4:17). After gathering some disciples to go with Him, we are told that "Jesus went about all Galilee, . . . preaching" (4:23). At the beginning of another tour of the land, Matthew reports that "he departed thence to teach and to preach in their cities

18

(11:1; compare Mark 1:38, 39). Jesus did this in fulfilment of the prophecy which said, "The Spirit of the Lord is upon me, because he hath anointed me to preach the gospel to the poor" (Luke 4:18).

(3) Preaching was central in the witness of the apostles. Immediately after the Ascension, Mark reports that the apostles "went forth, and preached every where (16:20). They had just been instructed by Jesus to "Go ye into all the world, and preach the gospel to every creature" (16:15). Paul's response and testimony was characteristic of these disciples. He said, "I was not disobedient unto the heavenly vision" (Acts 26:19).

Peter's sermon at Pentecost (Acts 2) is probably typical of the early preaching. So is that of Stephen in Acts 7. Such preaching during the next three centuries was to turn the world upside down and bring Christianity to be the foremost religion of the Roman Empire.

No substitute has been found for preaching. Where the power of preaching has waned, so has the spread of the saving movement. No great revival movement has ever arisen except where there has been a revival of the power of preaching. Luther and the Reformation; John Wesley and the great English revival; Whitefield, Wesley, and Jonathan Edwards in the Great Awakening in America; Spurgeon, Finney, Moody, and Sunday in other eras; these are just a few of the preachers associated with the power of the pulpit. These typify the need for preachers in every age.

19

C. THE MEANING OF HOMILETICS

Homiletics is a word that has been held in disdain by many. The study of homiletics has suggested the artificial style of the "educated" preacher. However, it is a term related closely to preaching and deserves a hearing as to its real meaning. It has had different meanings.

1. A simple talk. Its original meaning was to designate a simple talk or familiar discourse. This referred to an address which was not much more than simple conversation.

2. The art of preaching. A more formal definition has been "that theological science of which preaching is the art." So homiletics is a science which deals with (a) the purpose and nature of sermon building and delivery and (b) the skills and techniques of sermon building and delivery. So sermons and their delivery are the chief emphases of homiletics. These should be of interest to every man who plans to be a preacher.

3. Application of rules to sacred speech. In reality then homiletics is the application of sound rules of communication to sacred discourse. The preacher should study grammar and composition. Knowledge of language is vital to the most efficient communication. He should also familiarize himself with proper rules and techniques in speech. His voice is his tool. Proper speech techniques will not only protect his voice but will make him an able communicator of his message.

Phillips Brooks said, "Rules in homiletics are to be

helpful friends, not arrogant masters." This is good advice. In a study of both speech and language, the young preacher should avoid three things especially: (1) *Overemphasis on rules and forms.* These take personality out of preaching. An overly formal message is not attractive to a congregation. (2) *Imitation of other preachers.* The tendency in imitation is to copy the bad points of another preacher. In some areas of the country preachers have a nasal whang. Every young preacher who comes along feels that he has to attain that certain resonant sound or he is not preaching. This is bad. So are similar habits. (3) *Artificiality.* Whether it is stance, speech, or words, any artificiality in the speech or manner of the preacher tends to weaken his message. So, as Brooks advised, let rules be "helpful friends."

D. REASONS FOR HOMILETICAL STUDY

Though there are these dangers in homiletical studies, this should not keep him from applying himself to a study of the art of preaching. The reasons for study outweigh these minor dangers. Some of these are as follows:

1. Gratitude to God. Paul said, "I thank Christ Jesus our Lord, who hath enabled me, for that he counted me faithful, putting me into the ministry (1 Timothy 1:12). Every preacher should be thankful to God for his high calling. To be an ambassador for a king or president would indeed be an honor. But to be a spokesman for God, an announcer of His good news, is a supreme honor. Therefore, we should devote time to a study which would make us His most able spokesman.

2. *The Need for Strong Preaching.* The world is adept at spreading its philosophies. Men of the world utilize the greatest training facilities to prepare for the spread of their philosophies. To offset this, we need men who will give themselves devotedly to a study of the art of preaching. Solomon said, "Surely the serpent will bite without enchantment; and a babbler is no better" (Ecclesiastes 10:11). A serpent and a babbler need no training to do their harm. But the man of God needs to train his powers for the best presentation of his message.

3. *A Consciousness of Personal Limitations.* Some men have natural gifts that take them a long way in preaching. Most young preachers in their first sermons are praised whether they say anything or not. Blessed is the young man that can listen to such praise and not believe it. Most of us are woefully inadequate as communicators of our message when we begin speaking. A consciousness of limitations should spur us on to improve ourselves.

4. *The Desire to Be Effective.* To speak one hour to one man takes one hour of his time and one of yours. To speak to one hundred people for an hour consumes one hundred hours. Time so spent should be worthwhile. Only a speaker who has something to say and can say it deserves to consume that many man hours. An ineffective speaker is only beating the wind and wasting

time. The preacher's desire should be to become the most effective speaker possible.

There are several factors which will determine the value of the study of homiletics for each individual. Some of these are (1) a genuine love for the ministry, (2) a respect for and an awareness of the bigness of the preacher's task, (3) a willingness to pay the price of hard work, (4) a sense of need felt for help and a willingness to be helped, and (5) a willingness to give and receive criticism in sermons preached.

E. CHARACTERISTICS WHICH BRING EFFECTIVE PREACHING

Effective preaching results from the grace of God. But there is a human element involved also. There will be no effective preaching unless there is effort by the preacher. Some things that make the preacher effective are these.

1. The ability to prepare and deliver sermons according to some homiletical standard. This does not mean that one must have a college or seminary education. It does mean that somewhere and in some way the preacher adopts methods in preparation and delivery of sermons which allow him to put across his message. He may never go to school but he observes how some other effective preacher outlines his messages and he learns from him. Or, he may learn by experience how to prepare and deliver a message. But he develops

23

his talent so that he can prepare and deliver an effective message.

2. A study program out of which sermons grow. The old cliche that "God will fill you" is misunderstood. One old preacher added "with hot air." God will fill the preacher with power who studies and applies himself. He will give recall of Scriptures to a man who has diligently studied the Scriptures. The lazy preacher who does not study the Scriptures will never be given remembrance of them. He has nothing to remember.

The "workman that needeth not to be ashamed" is the one who diligently applies himself to study (2 Timothy 2:15). Such a one will be "throughly furnished unto all good works" (2 Timothy 3:17). He will always have a message to preach "in season, out of season" (4:2).

The testimony of many preachers is that they despise their study. They hate to be penned up in their offices. This shows in their preaching too. The thousands of preachers standing in pulpits around the world on Sunday morning represent one of the most vital forces in the world. How much of that power is made invalid because so many preachers do not pay the price of diligent study. Fervent prayer and a searching of the Scriptures precede effective preaching.

3. A life with spiritual depth. The life of the preacher is involved with spiritual things. His life even above the ordinary believer's must exemplify the fruit of the Spirit. The one who proclaims the message of God above all others must live according to that

24

message. Like Paul the preacher should be able to say, "Brethren, be followers together of me" (Philippians 3:17).

4. Preaching which comes from a shepherd heart. "Reprove, rebuke, exhort" (2 Timothy 4:2) is our command. But the harsher aspects of our ministry is to be done "with all longsuffering." The preacher is sometimes a pastor (Ephesians 4:11). The original meaning of pastor is *shepherd.* The task of the shepherd is to see to the total needs of his flock. After the example of the Chief Shepherd, the undershepherd needs to love his flock so that he will be willing to give his life for them.

5. A proper relationship to God, self, and others. The preacher generally is not called to be as John, a voice crying in the wilderness. He does not withdraw as a monk to a monastery. He is a man among men. He maintains his relationship to God while he lives among men. His relationship to other men is a demonstration that what he preaches can be lived in the everyday life of a believer. "A good report of them which are without" (1 Timothy 3:7) causes sinners to come to hear his message.

F. PERSONAL REQUISITES
TO EFFECTIVE PREACHING

These personal requisites overlap with some of the previous characteristics but bring home more forcibly to the preacher his needs.

1. Piety. "He's pious" has been used to reflect a low respect for someone. Actually it should never be used in this way. Of course, when it is used in this way, it is referring to false piety. True piety is a desired thing in a man of God. Piety is quality of soul. People should perceive a moral earnestness in the preacher which reflects a constant fellowship with God. His complete devotion to God should be reflected in a life filled with the Christian graces. A true piety will give power to his preaching.

2. Natural gifts. Broadus lists the natural gifts needed by a preacher as (1) clear thinking, (2) strong feelings, (3) a vigorous imagination, (4) a capacity for expression, and (5) the power of forcible expression. All natural gifts should be improved upon and developed by hard work.

3. Knowledge. The word *knowledge* is very prominent in Peter's second epistle (1:2, 3, 5, 6, 8; 3:18). The word refers to experience or experiential knowledge. The true preacher preaches from a depth of intimate knowledge of religious truth. Out of experience he has a knowledge of human nature and knows how to apply spiritual truth to life. The broader the preacher's knowledge, the more adept he can become in blessing the lives with which he comes in contact. He never ceases to be a student of religious truth and human nature. His knowledge becomes the material for his preaching and a means of applying it to lives.

4. Skills. Not all men are endowed with great and many natural gifts: "For ye see your calling, brethren, how that not many wise men after the flesh, not many mighty, not many noble, are called" (1 Corinthians 1:26). For this reason the preacher must develop skills. His style and delivery in preaching need careful cultivation. His choice and arrangement of preaching materials need refinement. Thoughtful practice and close observation of other speakers will enable a preacher to improve his own skills.

3

The Sermon

The communication of the preacher as delivered is usually referred to as a sermon. Sometimes it is referred to as a message. Let us here discuss it as a sermon.

A. THE DEFINITION OF A SERMON

The word *sermon* is derived from a Latin word which means "a stab, or a thrust." It apparently is a reference to a stabbing, piercing message. A. T. Pierson defined a sermon simply as "a speech spoken in behalf of, or in the name of God." One writer said that it is "an oral address to a general audience, with a view to unfolding, elaborating and enforcing scriptural truth." Gibbs quotes the definition given by Phelps who said, "A sermon is an oral address to the popular mind, upon scriptural truth contained in the Bible, elaborately treated and with a view to persuasion."

A sermon then is usually an oral, or spoken, address in contrast to written essays or articles. It is

28

spoken to people in general. Jesus' ministry was to "the people of the land" in contrast to the religious element in Jewry. His reason was: "They that be whole need not a physician, but they that are sick" (Matthew 9:12). The sermon is based on the truth contained in the Bible. The sermon presents a person. Jesus is the Truth of the Bible. Every sermon must present Him. The message is truth "elaborately treated." The preacher has closely examined the truth to be presented. His study resulted in a connected thought to bless his hearers. Persuasion is the goal of a sermon. Whether to salvation or to spiritual maturity, persuasion is behind every sermon.

B. THE PARTS OF THE SERMON

All writers do not agree as to the basic elements in a sermon. These are only listed here and will be presented in detail in later chapters. The parts are:
1. The text: the scriptural basis of the sermon.
2. The subject: the main truth to be expounded.
3. The introduction: that which introduces the subject.
4. The main body: the message as developed by the main points.
5. Illustrations: examples to enlarge understanding of the points.
6. The conclusion: the summation of arguments.
7. The invitation: the opportunity for response to the sermon.

29

C. TYPES OF SERMONS

The basic types of sermons are topical, textual, and expository. There are variations and blendings of these types and other types that will be discussed as special types.

1. The Topical Sermon

A topical sermon is one in which the subject or topic is prominent. Blackwood says that a topical sermon is "the unfolding of the subject with which the sermon begins." Pattison says, "Although the topical sermon is founded on some truth of Scripture, it differs from the textual sermon in that the topical formulates truth in the words of the preacher, the textual rather in the words of the Bible.

The topical sermon developed as a protest against the allegorical interpretation that prevailed in early centuries. Preaching became nothing more than verbal quibling and superstitious use of words. It was unscholarly and often misapplied the Scriptures. Early preachers like Chrysostom and Augustine used the topical method with no text.

Most of the great sermons in print are textual sermons. However, a trend has developed toward the use of expository and textual sermons.

The Advantages of Topical Sermons

1. The topical sermon allows the preacher to

preach on the subject he thinks needful for his people.
He can roam the Bible in search for a subject to meet
the needs of his congregation and passages to support it.
Pattison believes that the topical approach trains the
mind to breadth of view.

2. *Topical preaching allows for breadth and thoroughness of treatment.* The preacher can outline and
delineate the subject as he desires. He is not restricted
by the thought covered in one passage of Scripture.

3. *The topical sermon allows the preacher to make
for unity in his own way.* Textual and expository
sermons depend upon the unity already present in a
particular passage. When building a topical message, the
unity is developed by the preacher as he pleases.

4. *Topical preaching enables the preacher to use
and develop his oratorical, analytical, and literary
abilities to their greatest extent.* Care needs to be taken
lest the fruit of this advantage result in oratory rather
than in preaching.

5. *The topical approach permits the preacher to
develop his own means of reaching his goal.* This is one
of the most distinct advantages. The preacher can
develop his thought as he sees fit and arrive at his goal
as he prefers.

Disadvantages of Topical Preaching

1. *Topical preaching has a tendency to encourage
secularism in preaching.* It fosters the neglect of the
Word and stands as the opposite of Bible-centered

31

preaching. Liberalism with its emphasis on social issues has utilized topical preaching.

2. Topical preaching at times has a lack of human interest. Some preachers choose topics about which they enjoy reading and talking. These may not be of interest to the hearers. This writer recently saw a book by a layman. His cry was for preachers to preach the Word of God.

3. The number of topics is limited. A preacher will find his resources soon exhausted unless he is disciplined to hard study. Sermons are robbed of their variety and freshness unless the preacher really applies himself.

4. Topical preaching fosters a false concept of the purpose of preaching. Revivalism comes from the preaching of the Word of God. It is not good to preach about a passage of Scripture. The preacher is to open it up so that the hearer can receive the message of the Word.

Illustrations of Topical Sermons

There are many good topical sermons in print. Some outstanding ones are: "The Jerusalem Sinner Saved" by John Bunyan; "The Great Assize" (Romans 14:10c) by John Wesley; "The Character of Christ" (Matthew 17:5) by W. E. Channing; and "The God of the Aged" by Charles Spurgeon.

Some outlines copied for example are as follows:

HOW TO LIVE ABUNDANTLY

I. Learn Where the True Life Is (John 10:10).
II. Enter and Enjoy Abundant Living.
III. Explore the Possibilities of God-given Life (1 Corinthians 3:22, 23).

THE BEST IS YET TO BE
(1 Samuel 8:4-6)

This is a sermon to the middle-aged.

I. Accept the Fact that You Are Growing Older.
Go to the next step in life graciously.
II. Keep Making New Discoveries in Life.
Samuel was always eager for new discoveries and new experiences.
III. Seek Opportunities for Increasing Usefulness.
Some of life's greatest creations come from our elders.
IV. Maintain a Growing Experience with God (1 Samuel 12:23).

CHRISTIAN SELF-REALIZATION
(Romans 12:1)

I. Find Yourself.
II. Deny Yourself.
III. Accept Yourself.

Your limitations, weaknesses, strengths.
IV. Expose Yourself.
Enjoy Christian fellowship.
Enjoy Christ's company.
Witness to the world.

2. The Textual Sermon

The textual sermon is that sermon whose structure corresponds with or follows the parts in the text. The textual sermon deals with a short text usually not over one to three verses long. It follows closely the words of the text, phrase by phrase. It will not necessarily exhaust the meaning of the text, but it does confine itself to the meaning of the text. An outgrowth of textual preaching is a textual-topical message. This is one in which the sermon is expressed topically but treated textually.

Advantages of Textual Preaching

1. Textual preaching centers attention on one important passage of the Scriptures. It allows the preacher to press the meaning of a key thought. An example is Micah 6:8. This passage could be entitled "The Meaning of a Man's Religion." The points in the message would be obvious.

2. Textual sermons are not too difficult to prepare.

Of course, this is true if the preacher has chosen a good text which lends itself to textual development. Also it depends upon his willingness to develop the depth of its message. Micah 6:8 falls into three natural points. It is up to the preacher to explore and expound upon its truth.

3. *A textual sermon is easy for the people to follow.* If they have their Bible before them, they can watch as you unfold the riches of the chosen text.

4. *Textual preaching calls a preacher to prayer and Bible study.* He must be in a constant search for those gems of the Word which lend themselves to textual development. By prayerful search these will be found.

5. *Textual preaching assures a message from God when the preacher has the correct interpretation, presentation, and application.* It is Bible-based. It is up to the preacher to come through prayer and study to a correct interpretation. Then through diligent labor he is obligated to present it to his people and to apply it properly to their lives.

Disadvantages of Textual Preaching

1. *Every passage in the Bible cannot be developed as a textual sermon.* Those to be so used are those which are pithily stated and full of meaning. Not all are like John 3:16, Micah 6:8, or Isaiah 40:31 and fall into simple and clear divisions.

2. *A text may contain more ideas than a preacher*

can handle. He may have to go to topical preaching to develop each idea involved by a series of sermons.

3. Textual preaching can lead to mechanical preaching. It is not good for your people to learn how to anticipate how you are going to develop a text on Sunday after Sunday.

4. Like topical preaching, care must be taken lest a textual sermon should lack human interest. The preacher has the responsibility to illustrate his message with life's experiences.

Cautions about Textual Preaching

1. Choose your text with great care. Do not force points out of a text that are not in it.

2. Know what the text says and preach it. Do not be like the preacher who preached on "Diver's Diseases" from Matthew 4:24. (When church is over, they dive for the door. When someone isn't looking, they dive for the bottle, etc.)

3. Do not make a habit of using identical phrases or words of the text as an outline for the main body of the sermon. If you are not careful, the same words and phrases will make your people think they are hearing the same sermon every week.

4. Do not preach textual sermons to the exclusion of other types. Variety is the spice of life and variety in types of sermons will make your preaching spicier too.

Examples of Textual Sermons

THREE TIMES IN A NATION'S HISTORY
(Luke 19:41-44)

I. A Day of Grace, "This thy day."
II. A Day of Blindness, "hid from thine eyes."
III. A Day of Judgment, "thine enemies shall cast a trench about thee."

GREAT THINGS IN EPHESIANS 4:30

I. A Great Period—"day of redemption."
II. A Great Privilege—"sealed."
III. A Great Practical Requirement—"grieve not."
IV. A Great Persuasion to Performance of a Requirement—"grieve not the holy Spirit of God, whereby ye are sealed."

Below is a topical-textual treatment of 1 John 4:19.

I. A Fact Deserving Open Avowal.
   ("We love him.")
II. An Effect Flowing from a Cause.
   ("We love him because.")
III. A Simplicity Founded on a Mystery.
   ("He first loved us.")

37

IV. A Force Sustained by Another Force.
("We love him, because he first loved us.")

Instead of purely textual, giving emphasis to every point in a verse, particular points may be chosen for emphasis. Notice the use of three emphases from Hebrews 2:3 rather than all six.

I. A Mighty Deliverance ("so great salvation").
II. An Impending Danger ("neglect").
III. An Inevitable Doom ("how shall we escape").

3. The Expository Sermon

The Meaning of Expository Preaching

The literal meaning of exposition is to put forth or set out the meaning. When applied to preaching, it refers to the exposing or setting out of the meaning of the Scriptures. One definition given is "the textual treatment of a longer passage of Scripture than is used in textual preaching—the main parts of the body of the sermon being drawn from the passage of Scripture." Another writer has said that it is "exposing a more lengthy passage of Scripture properly, orderly, and with a view of persuading people to act upon it." The major divisions and at least the first subdivisions are drawn from this relatively long passage of Scripture.

Whitesell, in his book, lists seven factors in expository preaching:

1. It is based on a passage in the Bible, either short or long.

2. It seeks to learn the primary, basic meaning of that passage.

3. It relates that meaning to the context of that passage.

4. It digs down for the timeless, universal truths stemming out of the passage.

5. It organizes these truths around one central theme.

6. It uses the rhetorical elements of explanation, argument, illustration, and application to bring the truth of the passage home to the hearer.

7. It seeks to persuade the listeners to obey the truth of the passage discussed.

Important in a definition of expository preaching is what it is not. It is not the mere reading of a portion of Scripture and making comment on it. That fallacy leads to weak preaching. True expository preaching is powerful, informative, and challenging. This is a distinct type of sermonizing in which it is possible to maintain unity, orderly progress, and logical sequence.

There are several things which should be noted about expository preaching.

1. The majority of preachers would admit that expository preaching is the best method. They may not use it often, but they admit that it is the epitomy of preaching.

2. It is generally agreed that this has been a much neglected method of preaching. "Three points and an illustration" for a brief inspirational message has been the style in recent years while the great Biblical passages with depth go neglected.

3. There has not been a lot of help available for men who desired to become great expository preachers. A few more books have appeared in recent years, and more helps are beginning now to come on the market.

Advantages of Expository Preaching

1. There is scriptural precedent for expository preaching. Jesus used it (Luke 4:16-21). This seems to have been the original plan. The messages of the apostles were filled with the Scriptures (Acts 8:35).

2. Exposition is the most natural way of presenting the truth of the Scriptures. It is the direct method. It is truly "preaching the Word."

3. It demands a greater knowledge of the Bible on the part of the preacher. At the same time it produces a better knowledge on the part of the people. As he is incited to study, so he builds them up in knowledge of the divine truth. Since he must stick so close to the Word, it reduces any temptation to misinterpret and misapply the Scriptures.

4. Expository preaching gives opportunity to make practical admonitions that might otherwise seem overly personal. For example, in a topical message the person listening might think that you designed your admonitions with him in mind. In expository preaching you can show how something happened to a Bible character; then you can say, so it may happen to you.

5. *Expository preaching may utilize a variety of types of exposition.* Generally speaking a complete passage is used. However, the preacher may choose to do an exposition of only the important words or phrases in a passage. References to a person may be grouped to form a biographical sermon. There are times that a preacher may develop a course or series of sermons on the entire Bible or a single book. He could use the parables or the miracles to develop a series of expositions. By using such a variety he does not develop a monotonous pattern.

Expository sermons are not easily prepared. The choice of the proper passage, the making of application to everyday life, and other difficulties will be met. The preacher who has success in expository preaching needs the following qualifications: (1) an intelligent faith in the inspiration of the Scriptures; (2) a power of selection; (3) a logical mind; (4) real preaching power; and (5) studious habits that are constantly maintained.

Examples of Expository Sermons

A simple outline by Henry Drummond on a single chapter:

THE GREATEST THING IN THE WORLD
(1 Corinthians 13)

I. The Importance of Love (verses 1-3).
II. The Characteristics of Love (verses 4-7).
III. The Permanence of Love (verses 8-13).

An example of a sermon on a whole book, the Book of Jonah:

MODERN JONAHS
(Jonah 4:10, 11)

I. The Historical Setting of the Book
II. The Contents of the Book.
III. The Permanent Message of the Book.
   A. How little we learn from our social misfortunes.
   B. How desperately we try to escape God's call to the highest.
   C. How stubbornly we refuse to accept the lostness of man.
   D. How difficult it is to believe in a God of love for lost man.

An example of an expository sermon by the interrogative method is shown in this outline in Romans 5:1-11:

42

JUSTIFICATION

I. What Is Justification?
II. What Are Its Blessings?
III. When Do We Have Them?

An outline of Whitesell's on the praying widow of Luke 18:1-8 yields these points:

I. She prayed persistently (verse 3).
II. She prayed definitely (verse 3).
III. She prayed earnestly (verses 3, 5).
IV. She prayed believingly (verses 3-7).

4. Special Types of Sermons

There are many and varied types of sermons. Some might be classified as *occasional*. Under this classification would fall those sermons at Thanksgiving and Easter, on special patriotic days, at gatherings such as a PTA meeting, or on any other occasion which is not regular.

A doctrinal series of messages would be a special type. So would a series of ethical messages enforcing personal duties and right living. Some preachers have used historical messages either from the Bible or from church history. The latter is fine as long as they remain true to the Scriptures. Experimental or experiential messages stimulate, comfort, correct, and instruct. These too should be built upon the Scriptures.

Characteristics of Special Sermons

1. Make them fit the time allowed for the message. A long winded preacher who cannot keep within the bounds of his allotted time is never appreciated. Many good messages have lost their effect by the preacher's failure to observe his time limits. To be put on a program at a special occasion is an honor and an opportunity. Do not ruin the opportunity by running over time.

2. Preach the heart of the gospel whatever the occasion. There may be someone there who will hear the gospel nowhere else. Count it a high privilege and work the basic gospel message into your sermon. You can do this whatever the occasion and whatever your assigned topic may be.

3. Make them full of Christ. After all, the only reason you have been invited to speak is because you are His ambassador. An ambassador presents the one who sent him. Make your hearers well aware of the one you represent.

4. Seek through every special sermon to awaken and encourage to salvation. It is on special occasions when we preach the special type sermons that we are facing an audience of unsaved more than usual. They need to be reminded of their need. Your message might prick their consciences and cause them to seek salvation.

44

Some Suggestions for Revival Sermons

1. Make the message short and pithy. Since you may have a long after-service, plan your message so that it is not too long. Like Eutychus even sinners go to sleep after so long.

2. Vary the character and content of the different messages. Variety in both character and content will result in a greater effect upon your listeners.

3. Develop some form of sequence to follow. Each message should build upon and support the previous one. By this method a growing impact will fall upon your hearers.

4. Avoid sensationalism and vulgar denunciation. Depend more upon the Holy Spirit to make your message effective than you do upon your own antics. The Holy Spirit can bring greater condemnation through the truth than you can through harsh words.

5. Preach a sound, thorough, and complete message. Your revival preaching should be on basic truths. These should be clearly expounded. Such will have longer and greater effect than sensational topics and lightly presented sermons.

4
The Text

In this and the next five chapters the parts of the sermon will be discussed. Each part is vital in the construction of the sermon. Study each one carefully.

A. THE MEANING OF THE TEXT

Most descriptions of sermons begin with the words: "He took his text from." The text is one of the chief elements in distinguishing a sermon from other types of oral address. Its meaning should be examined closely by every preacher.

1. Its Historical Meaning. The idea of the text arose as the work of some author was read. As the speaker spoke he often made notes in the side margins or at the bottom of the page which he used to make his own comments. The work of the original author was referred to as the *text* to distinguish it from the speaker's notes.

The earliest preaching was a running comment on a text. A preacher would read the Scriptures and make comment. What he read from the Scriptures was called his *text*. This was to distinguish it from the preacher's remarks which were the sermon.

In time the comments of the preacher were lengthened upon a certain section. The sermon part grew as the speaker's comments became more lengthy. As shorter passages came to serve as the basis of the comments, it continued to be referred to as the text.

2. The Literal Meaning. The word *text* is from a Latin word which means to weave. The ideas, to put together and to construct, are derived from this basic meaning. The text came to refer to something woven into the entire web of the discourse. The text commands the structure of the whole sermon. It is not a starting point or something to introduce the sermon. It refers to a portion of the Scriptures which permeates the whole message.

3. The Practical Meaning. A. W. Blackwood said that the text is "the Biblical source of the sermon." The definition given by Broadus is similar. He called it "the portion of Scripture chosen as the foundation for a sermon." This meaning of a text reminds the preacher that he is not undertaking to give his own wisdom; rather, he is trying to impart an understanding of the Word of God. The taking of a text affords him the opportunity of explaining and impressing upon the minds of the hearer some portion of the Word.

B. CHOOSING A TEXT

Someone has well said, "Texts should never be

47

chosen just to please self, but to glorify God and to meet some human need." This is so true. Neither the novelty of some text nor the fascination of a text, but only the opportunity to present a message from God, should dictate the choice of a text. Some factors to guide the preacher in choosing a text need to be noted.

Guiding Factors in Choosing a Text

1. The preacher's personality. Preachers differ in many ways. Talents, abilities, and other personal elements will dictate the text chosen by an individual preacher. These differences ensure that the whole message of God is presented. If all were alike and chose the same texts, how monotonous sermons would be!

2. The preacher's general preparation and knowledge of the Bible. Sometimes it appears that the most unprepared and inexperienced preachers choose the most difficult texts. Ability to handle a text should enter into the choice of a text for a message. Young preachers should avoid difficult texts until they are able to handle them.

3. The preacher's prayer life. Impressions for sermons will grow out of a preacher's prayer life and devotional life. Impressions here will override other considerations.

4. The preacher's knowledge of people and community, national, and world affairs. There should always be a relationship between the choice of a text and the need of people. Often current happenings among people will call for certain subjects to be preached.

5. *The church program.* Soul winning programs, missions emphases, stewardship responsibilities, and other church programs will often suggest texts to be utilized.

6. *Current religious topics.* What others are preaching will often influence your preaching. A new emphasis on evangelism in recent years has prompted preaching on evangelistic texts. Such things as the "God Is Dead" issue often spur a lot of preaching on texts to contradict them.

7. *Refusal of some texts to let you go.* The preacher who lives in a constant study of the Bible will find that certain texts will capture his mind and refuse to let it go. When a text gets such a grip on you and thrills you, you can often make it a blessing to your people.

8. *Special requests.* Members will sometimes ask you to preach on certain texts. Beware of these unless you can feel the definite leadership of the Lord in the use of a text. Remember the burden for a message must come from Him.

Caution in Choosing a Text

1. *Be sure the text is clear to you or that its meaning becomes clear to you.* When a text thrills a preacher, he often preaches from it on the basis of

inspiration rather than study. It is embarrassing to preach on a text and to find out later that a wrong interpretation has been given to it. A text unclear to you will never yield a clear message to your people.

2. Be cautious about humorous texts. A humorous text may delight your audience, but usually the humor is retained in the mind rather than a message from God.

3. Avoid choosing texts from only one section of the Bible. Some preachers choose texts only from the New Testament to the exclusion of the Old Testament. Others get bogged down in the delightful epistles of Paul while neglecting the gospels, Acts, and other writings. This is not good. Use texts from Genesis to Revelation.

4. Avoid the sayings of uninspired men as if they were truth. "There is no God" is a quote from the Bible, but it is the word of the fool (Psalm 53:1). "All is vanity" is a statement from the worldly man's viewpoint (Ecclesiastes 1:2). Gamaliel's advice sounds good, but it was the advice of an uninspired man (Acts 5:33-39). If such texts are used, be sure to explain their origin.

Texts Not To Be Avoided

1. Familiar texts. John 3:16, Acts 1:8, Matthew 28:18-20 and other familiar texts if avoided would become unfamiliar to our children and new converts. While not avoiding them, the preacher should make sure that he gives a new freshness to them when he does use them.

50

2. Difficult texts. Yes, the young, or newly called, preacher should avoid them. But the seasoned preacher must declare "the whole counsel of God." As he grows in his knowledge and understanding of the Bible, the preacher should open all the texts that he can to his congregation.

3. Evangelistic texts. Some pastors feel inadequate to speak on the great evangelistic texts. This is indeed a fallacy. The pastor is obligated to press the claims of the great evangelistic texts regularly.

4. Doctrinal and ethical texts. These may not be as popular and as inspirational as some texts, but they need to be preached. A congregation unfounded in the great doctrines and untaught in Christian ethics and morals will be a weak people in spiritual things.

Suggestions for Finding Texts

1. Read your Bible daily. A constant reading of the Bible will result in the constant finding of passages that stand out in your mind. Verses, even in the more familiar gospels, will grasp your mind as never before when you reread them.

2. Keep on the search for texts. Do not just read. Analyze verses as you read them. Ask yourself, "Are there principles of truth in these verses that need exposition to my people?"

3. Observe the needs of your people. Get out among people. Talk with them. Sense their needs. Then the Holy Spirit will reveal Scriptures from your reading that will fill their needs.

4. Pray much in your study. Prayer, Bible study, and the search for texts go hand in hand. Do not neglect to relate your prayer life to your study.

C. HOW TO STUDY TEXTS

A text needs to be studied before one goes into the preparation of the sermon. This is to ensure that the meaning of the text is clear to the preacher. An understanding of the text will aid in the preparation of the message. Of course, in a textual sermon, elaboration on the text is the message.

Four basic steps should be taken in the study of the text.

1. Read the text in various versions. The preacher should have versions other than the King James Version for study even though he never takes them to the pulpit. Read the other versions to see how it has been variously translated. Some fuller concept of its meaning may be gleaned from these.

2. Study the text in other languages. The study of the original Hebrew and Greek is ideal. For preachers who have never studied these languages, there are helps in these languages in some concordances (Young's and Strong's) and in many of the commentaries. For preachers who have studied French, German, Spanish, or other languages, study in these languages is good and enlightening.

3. Consider the whole context of the portion to be used as a text. It is good in the case of short books to gain a knowledge of the whole book. Begin, of course, with the immediate verse or verses under consideration. Read and study them carefully; then move to a study of the paragraph in which the text is found. After this enlarge your study to involve the whole chapter in which it is located. Remember that the full meaning of any text will be found by a study of its whole context. It is not right to lift a text out of its context and to use it as a proof text.

The meaning of major words in both text and context should be mastered well. The preacher should have lexicons, concordances, and word study books in his library for this use. Dictionaries and commentaries are useful in word studies also. By comparing what various writers say, one can come to his own decision about the meaning of words. Helps can also be found in good sermons by other preachers.

D. INTERPRETATION OF TEXTS

The text chosen for a sermon must be interpreted carefully. The correct interpretation can be reached by careful investigation. There are four areas that need careful investigation.

1. The historical background. There are several questions that the preacher needs to ask in regard to each passage being considered as a text. His general knowledge may already contain the answer to most of these. If not, he should seek the answer through research. Here are some questions to ask.

> a. Who was the writer?
> > (1) What was the situation at the time of the writing?
> > Does that situation influence the text?
> > (2) What is the temperament and the style of the author?
> b. Who were the readers intended?
> > (1) What was their situation?
> > (2) How did that influence the writer?
> c. What was the relationship between the author and readers?
> d. Are there any facts of geographical significance?
> e. Are there any political and governmental situations of significance? (Who was the Roman emperor or the Judean king? or the pharaoh of Egypt? or similar questions.)

As an example of the importance of these questions, study the readers for which the four gospels were intended. Matthew was originally written to a Hebrew or Jewish people, hence all the quotations from the Old Testament by which He is shown to be Israel's Promised King. Note the specific tracing of Jesus back to

Abraham. In Luke His genealogy is traced back to Adam and He is pictured as the Ideal Man, possibly as a message to Gentiles. These facts help explain many things recorded by these two authors.

   2. *Matters of literary interest.*
   a. Define the important words and key terms in the text.
      (1) Use commentaries and dictionaries.
      (2) Check references in concordances to get meaning from the usage of the terms elsewhere.
   b. Analyze the grammatical relations.
      (1) Diagram the sentences in the text. Know what your subject and predicate are and how other words are related to each other.
      (2) Look for the author's devices of emphasis. Often commentaries point these out. They are noticeable in the original language.
      (3) Look for play on tenses.
      (4) Note the antecedents of words.
   c. Check on figures of speech and understand them.
   d. Look for passages of comparable interest. Remember that the authority for interpretation of a passage is its comparison to other Scriptures. Each passage is to be interpreted in accord with the general teaching of the Scriptures.
   e. Check the context of the text.
      (1) Immediate context (paragraph).
      (2) General context (chapter or book).

3. The doctrinal viewpoint. Ask what the passage teaches. It is good to list those teachings on paper.

4. The practical implications. How does this text relate to the lives of your listeners? What are the key applications that you want to make to their lives?

Generally speaking, the preacher should confine himself to a strict interpretation of the text. Many preachers become guilty of misusing the text and by their actions reflect upon the integrity of other preachers. There are four common ways that texts are misused.

1. By careless or loose interpretation. Verses or phrases from the Scriptures are interpreted to accommodate the subject of discussion. One preacher is said to have spoken to a group of tailors on the thought: "A remnant shall be saved" (Romans 9:27). This is a false application because the "remnant" has nothing to do with a tailor's remnant. Sometimes literal expressions in texts are used figuratively in a forced way. One preacher is said to have used the idea of "a sepulchre in the midst of a beautiful garden" from John 19:41 to preach on sin in a beautiful life. In reality this accommodation based on a metaphorical expression does not give a very good basis for a message. Every time some preachers see "woman" in the Bible, they take it to be symbolic of the church. How absurd!

2. By giving multiple meanings to a text. For lack of a better knowledge, some give multiple meanings to texts. Remember that there is one meaning (possibly several applications) and you are searching for that one

56

meaning. A good example is John 3:5 which has the phrase, "born of water and of the Spirit." Its one meaning needs to be sought.

3. *By misunderstanding the phraseology of the text.* Language is easily misunderstood. This is especially true when words are not defined properly. This author once heard a preacher speak on the "Republican and the Sinner." Phraseology is sometimes misunderstood because the preacher fails to correctly analyze grammatical relations and constructions. At times the context of the text is either misinterpreted or disregarded. This is done because a preacher had rather allegorize than to study. At other times it results from a misunderstanding caused by chapter and verse divisions. Ignore these when you are studying the context of a passage.

4. *By allegorizing.* To allegorize means to assign a figurative meaning to a literal passage. It can also mean pressing the meaning of a figurative passage beyond what it is intended to portray. Whenever a preacher intends to allegorize, he should tell his listeners that he is not giving the real meaning but intends to use the passage as a figurative picture. John 5:1-5 does not picture sick Christians. However, a preacher can allegorize on the passage and use it as a picture of sick Christians *if he tells his listeners* that he is only using them in a figurative way. "Them that are at ease in Zion" (Amos 6:1) are often taken to be lazy folks in the church. Literally they are not. When so used, the preacher should let it be known that he is allegorizing.

57

Another illustration of misapplied texts is Colossians 2:21 which says: "Touch not; taste not; handle not." A look at the context will show that Paul was *condemning* not *commending* such rules. The "youth" of Timothy (1 Timothy 4:12) is often stressed because of misunderstanding. At the time Paul wrote to him he was definitely in the "over thirty" group.

There are times the preacher can depart from strict interpretation of the text. Here are some exceptions to the rule of sticking to the real meaning of a text.

1. A principle found in a text with one application may be used in another application. An example would be Paul's statement that "if meat make my brother to offend, I will eat no flesh while the world standeth" (1 Corinthians 8:13). Here is a principle given in regard to meat that can be applied in scores of other situations.

2. A general admonition is sometimes given that can be applied to a specific thing. "Prove all things" (1 Thessalonians 5:21) is a general admonition. A preacher could apply it to something in particular and say, "Test this by the Bible before you do it." In the next verse, "Abstain from all appearance of evil," is a general admonition. The command could be applied to a particular thing that gives an "appearance of evil."

3. A preacher may begin with some precise meaning in a text and proceed to a related truth. When Amos said, "Prepare to meet thy God," he was speaking of facing temporal judgment. The preacher can begin here

58

and proceed to warn people to prepare for the final judgment.

The preacher is obligated to use a text and to use it properly. Jesus used a text (Luke 4:20). Paul used a text (Acts 13:15). The messages of the apostles were saturated with the Scriptures. The people want and need a Biblical basis for what they are going to hear. Since we are called to "preach the word," the Lord expects us to use a text. But the very fact that we are dealing with the Word of God places that heavy responsibility upon the preacher to use the text properly.

5
The Subject

A. THE MEANING OF THE SUBJECT

Gibbs describes the subject as "the most striking truth contained in the text." This is good because it allows the text or scriptural basis to remain the controlling factor in the sermon. Broadus would not require a sermon to have a text but insists upon a subject. Many preachers reverse this and have only a text which doubles for a subject. Broadus thinks of the subject as "some significant truth bearing on religious life."

The sermon must have a text and each one will have a subject whether it is announced or not. Often the mere reading of the text will suggest the subject. There has been some question as to whether or not the subject must be announced. The masters of the pulpit have generally announced their subjects. One prominent exception was the great G. Campbell Morgan. It is good for the audience to hear an announced subject. They know the direction of the message. The announcing of the subject can serve as a check on the preacher also. It helps keep him from rambling.

There are advantages that result from having a specific subject. It ensures arrangement. What the preacher develops from the text should be in keeping with the announced text. It also promotes unity. As he announces the subject, so he brings out the relationship of each point to the subject. The subject is to be used distinctly throughout the message. It is to so rule the message that it is the final and dominant thought expressed by the preacher.

Subjects like texts may be classified in various ways. Broadus gives four classifications: *doctrinal*, the scriptural teaching on great truths; *subjects of morality*, exhortations to works and holiness; *historical*, the movement of God in history and the responses of the people; and *experimental*, the actual experiences of men in receiving the gospel and living its precepts.

B. ITS FORM AND CHARACTERISTICS

The form and characteristics of a subject are related and will be dealt with together under this heading.

The Form of the Subject

Three basic things should be said about the form of the subject:

1. The subject should be stated in a phrase rather than in a word or a sentence. A sentence tells the whole story. One word, such as "redemption," does not delimit the idea enough. But a phrase suggests more than it says.

2. The subject should be phrased in the preacher's own words. A teacher in reading a pupil's theme can detect what is the student's work and what is copied work. Oftentimes a preacher will borrow a subject that does not fit his vocabulary and personality and this fact is noticed by his listeners.

3. The subject form should vary from time to time. Give the people variety even in the manner of announcement of the subject. The subject should arouse interest in the message. If it is announced in the same form from time to time, it will lose its effectiveness.

Characteristics of the Subject

Four basic characteristics should mark each subject. The preacher should work on the wording of each subject so that it will be so characterized.

1. Clearness. Clarity in thought and wording is to be the goal. Though the thought is clear to the preacher, he should labor so that the words used to express the subject make it clear to his hearers. If they do not understand the subject, it will be doubtful that they understand the message.

2. Propriety. Avoid remote and untimely subjects.

Your subject should fit the time and the occasion. It should have a present application to the immediate audience. Most have heard the old illustration of the deacons who did not like their pastor's messages that touched their lives. Finally they told him to "Preach on Indians. There isn't one within five hundred miles." Do not choose subjects unless they are applicable to the lives of your hearers.

3. Freshness. Express your topic in a new and refreshing way. Read sermon topics by outstanding preachers and notice how they use the great old truths of the Bible but express them in attractive, fresh ways.

4. Sufficiency. The subject should fully cover what you are going to express in your sermon. Define the boundaries of your message by wording the subject properly. Do not make it so broad that your specific emphasis is not given.

C. SOURCES OF THE SUBJECT

There are many sources for subjects. Just a few will be mentioned here.

1. The Bible. As previously mentioned, the subject may be contained in the text. The exact words from the text should not be used too often. The subject may be logically inferred from the text by way of induction from a particular statement to a general thought. A good example would be the subject, "The Futility of Covetousness," based on Luke 19:19, 20.

The opposite can also be a source. By way of induction a subject of a specific nature can be chosen from a general admonition. An example of this could be from Romans 12:9. The exhortation to "abhor that which is evil" could be used for the subject, "Abhor the Evil of Pornography."

The subject may just be suggested by the text. The subject, "Taking Account of Small Things," was used based on Genesis 1:6.

2. The subject may be assigned.

3. The subject may be suggested by the place and the occasion. A homecoming, a memorial service, or a service of some special type would demand a related subject.

4. Subjects may be suggested as a result of needs sensed as you make pastoral calls.

5. Your general reading may remind you of a subject to be used.

6. Current events will often remind you of a Biblical truth that needs to be presented.

D. THE WORDING OF THE SUBJECT

Several factors will influence each preacher's wording of his subject. Not every preacher will follow the same pattern of wording as other preachers. Four of these factors are listed here.

1. The preacher's vocabulary. Preachers differ in vocabulary. The words used by a preacher should be

64

words that he can use with facility. A friend of the writer loved to learn and use new words. His problem was that he often used them before he knew their precise meaning. One's ignorance shows through when this happens.

2. The people's vocabulary. The preacher should know the capability of his audience to understand words. Never use language beyond their understanding.

3. The preacher's imagination. Some preachers have a rich imagination and can think up attractive and interesting subjects. This gives an added element to any sermon.

4. The preacher's purpose. Your purpose in the sermon will dictate the wording of the subject. An inspirational address will have a lighter subject than one delivered on a more formal occasion. A more serious subject would be given to a sermon preached at a large convention than one preached at the ordinary evening service in your church.

E. A STANDARD OF MEASUREMENT

Here are some suggestions based on the suggestions by A. W. Blackwood.

1. A subject should be interesting and attractive but not overly sensational. A subject becomes sensational when it calls attention to itself and the preacher rather than to Christ and the gospel. "Seven Ducks in a Muddy Stream" (2 Kings 5:10) seems somewhat sensational. So does "A Baptist Preacher who Lost His head at a Dance" (Mark 6:27).

2. A subject should be clear but not so revelatory that it details the preacher's ideas. It should only suggest his line of thought.

3. A subject should be short, but not abrupt. The ideal subject will have only two to four strong words in it. "Faith" is too broad. "The Significance of Faith" is good. "The Tremendous Implications of Unfaltering Trust in the Omnipotent Ruler of the Cosmic Order" is too long and complicated.

4. The subject should have a rhythmical sound but not to the point of excess. Some subjects that are properly marked by rhythm are: "Pilgrim's Progress," "The Jerusalem Sinner Saved," and "Grace Abounding to the Chief of Sinners."

5. The subject should be accurate but not so precise that your listeners feel that you are parading or displaying your learning. People in the average congregation resent any display of scholarship. Just make your subject accurate enough to include all that will be in the sermon.

6. A subject should be religious and not too much "this worldly." The subject should suggest religion. The use of movie titles, television titles, or other secular or worldly oriented thoughts are dangerous because they blend the spiritual with the worldly. It is especially not good to have a title even suggestive of some of the more sordid titles from the world.

7. A subject should sound familiar to the people while not being fully comprehended by them. Something should be left for their anticipation.

8. *A subject should not clash with the moral life of the preacher.* A preacher who preaches on tithing should tithe. A preacher who preaches against drugs should not be hooked on nicotine.

9. *The subject should be vital to the needs of the people.* When a preacher enters the pulpit, he should feel, "I've got something I must tell you."

10. *A subject should be in keeping with the time allowed for the message.* Some subjects cannot be dealt with in twenty-five minutes. When limited by time, delimit the subject according to the time allotted.

6

The Introduction

The introduction is the first part of the sermon presented to the hearers. It would follow the reading of the text and statement of the subject, or it could involve either or both of these.

A. THE MEANING OF THE INTRODUCTION

The introduction consists of several statements to lead into the sermon. A prelude to a poem or piece of music creates a desired atmosphere for what is to follow. So should an introduction. The preface to a book offers high suggestions as to what is to follow and builds anticipation for the general content of a book. So should an introduction leave the listener with anticipation for the rest of the sermon. A porch on a house is merely the entrance way to something better. An introduction should promise much better things to come in the sermon. It is a doorway that leads into the presentation of something vital to the lives of your audience.

The introduction is highly significant. It is during these first moments of the sermon that the preacher will either get or lose his audience. To lose them in the introduction can be and is usually fatal to the whole sermon.

B. THE PURPOSE OF THE INTRODUCTION

Too many preachers spend all of their time building the main body of their sermon and give little time to their introduction. They leave the introduction to the inspiration of the moment (which often falls flat). However, many outstanding preachers have realized the importance of the introduction and have prepared it well. When one realizes the purpose of the introduction, it will cause him to prepare it well. Let us note its purpose.

1. The introduction should draw attention to the text and subject of the sermon. The intent of the sermon and its basis in the Scriptures should become well imprinted upon the minds of the hearers through the introduction.

2. The introduction is intended to arouse both mental and spiritual interest. It should have in it elements to awaken mental perception and to quicken spiritual thoughts. Only when it so stimulates the hearer has it performed its purpose.

3. The introduction should be given in a manner to secure favor for the preacher. Only when an audience respects you will they respect your message. Your audience may be prejudiced toward you and your subject. Make a favorable impression during your introduction. At least, do not further antagonize them. Study Peter's introduction in Acts 2:14-21; Stephen's in Acts 7:2; and some of Paul's in Acts 13:16-23; 17:22, 23; 22:1-5; 26:1-3.

4. *The introduction should bring the preacher and the people together.* Their minds may be elsewhere. You must bring them from where they are to rivet them on the subject at hand. Clear away the obstacles that would keep their thoughts from listening to and considering your message.

C. MARKS OF A GOOD INTRODUCTION

Good introductions do not just happen. They are the result of thought and planning. Several characteristics should mark a good introduction.

1. *It should be interesting and suggestive.* Depart from the usual "preachy" introduction. Put your thoughts over in a fresh way. An interesting introduction builds anticipation for your sermon.

2. *It should be marked by unity.* Have only one central, unified thought in your introduction. Avoid a double approach. It will consume too much time and will tend to confuse your hearers. The introduction should be singular, leading directly to the main body.

3. *It should be brief and to the point.* Five minutes at the most should be devoted to the introduction. A fifteen or twenty minute introduction is a sermon itself.

Quit if you go that long. Save the sermon for another occasion.

4. *A good introduction is marked by simplicity.* The idea should build gradually to a climax. It should not be complicated and in need of a lot of explanation and illustration.

5. *A good introduction gives the appearance of being natural.* Have it memorized. Do not make references to your notes. In a clear, calm, and deliberate manner give your introduction without an appearance of grasping for something to say. Avoid exaggeration and keep it somewhat conversational.

6. *A good introduction is marked by clarity.* The introduction is no place for the deep and the profound. A clear, precise statement in your introduction will avoid confusion.

7. *A good introduction should be carefully prepared.* The audience should sense that what you have to say is worthy of their attention. Any indication that you are unprepared will cause you to lose your audience.

8. *A good introduction will be pertinent.* It should clearly indicate your line of thought. A pertinent introduction will be closely related to your subject and lead into the theme of the main body.

D. THINGS TO AVOID

Several things should be avoided in an introduction. Here are a few suggestions.

1. Avoid apologies in your introduction. Two types of apologies are most often heard: for one's health and for one's preparation. This writer remembers one preacher in particular whose basic introduction was: "I feel bad. I shouldn't be here. I'm about to pass out." The resultant feeling to the listeners was: "Why didn't you stay in bed?"

Do not apologize for lack of preparation. The congregation will know it as you proceed, so save your breath. Neither should you apologize for your subject. If the Lord did not lay it on your heart, don't preach it. If the Lord did lay it on your heart, don't apologize for it.

Likewise, apologizing for your appearance or dress or similar things only calls attention to them. It is better to avoid getting your people's minds on these things.

2. Avoid using a part of the main body of the sermon as part of the introduction. If you use a part of the main body in the introduction and then use it again, the listeners will become conscious of your repetition. It also will weaken the effect in your main body.

3. Avoid elaborate readings and quotes. A single quote may serve well as an introduction. Anything drawn out is prohibited by all good rules of speech.

4. Avoid strong expressions of personal feelings at this point. This may be all right later. Present your arguments before your conclusions.

5. Avoid antagonizing your audience in the introduction. As already stated, what you want now is their attention and acceptance. Any animosity toward you at this point voids your message.

E. TYPES OF INTRODUCTION

Introductions should vary from sermon to sermon. The preacher should study various types of introduction which he may use. Here are some possibilities.

1. Textual. Elaborate on the setting and intent of the text. Then briefly interpret the text and show its relationship to your subject and the whole sermon. (Remember, do not preach a part of your main body here.)

2. Contextual. Explain the setting of the chapter or paragraph (or sometimes the whole book) from which the text is taken. The context may stress the *scene.* For example, a message from the Sermon on the Mount might be introduced by a description of the scene there by the Sea of Galilee. A message from John 10 on the Good Shepherd might describe the *situation* of the shepherd caring for his flock. The bibliography of a prominent person in a passage would serve as a basis for a good introduction. An example would be Timothy when preaching from one of his books. A great truth in a passage might be used. An example is Luke 15 (the lost sheep, the lost coin, the lost son).

3. Topical. Develop your introduction topically. The topic, of course, would be related to the main body and an introduction to it.

4. Dramatic. Preachers with a gift for drama could use some type dramatic production to introduce an occasional message.

5. A striking quotation. A striking quotation from the Bible or some other source can be used very effectively to get attention and to introduce the message.

6. A statement of purpose. The statement of your purpose in the sermon and a description of your approach to the sermon makes a good introduction. In stating your purpose, remember that you are not to tell all in the introduction that you intend to develop in the main body of the sermon.

7. Illustration. An illustration may be used, but keep in mind that the illustration is to introduce only. An illustration or illustrations that lead into the development of the subject are appropriate, but not those that develop your subject.

Avoid humorous introductions. These tend to give a levity to the whole message if not handled carefully. The introduction should suggest the gravity of the message. Also just a general statement should be avoided as an introduction. Be specific and to the point in what you have to say.

F. SOURCES OF INTRODUCTION

The Bible is your source book for texts so is therefore unlimited. Subjects may come from the whole range of Biblical and theological learning, as well as practical spiritual experience. But the sources of the introduction are much more limited. The introduction for the individual sermon will be restricted by your text, your subject, and the occasion. Of course, the whole range for all introductions will be just as broad as that of texts, subjects, and occasions.

Since the introduction is the bridge between the text and the main body, it must be related to your text and the subject to be developed. Either as an enlargement upon the text or the announced subject, it demonstrates the relation of these to the main body of the sermon. There will be times when the occasion may dominate the introduction. However, in such cases the subject is usually in keeping with the occasion.

7

The Main Body of the Sermon

The main body is the basic sermon itself. It is here that the preacher interprets the message of God to His people and to those who should become His people. This part of the sermon is called the discussion by Gibbs. It is in the main body that the truth contained in the text and subject are presented. Through some plan which he has developed, the preacher will through logical sequence develop the various aspects of his message. Like one breaking bread for hungry people, the preacher breaks the Word of Life for the awaiting congregation. His message is to be so constructed that they perceive the great truths in the Word.

A. MARKS OF A GOOD SERMON BODY

Several things should characterize a good sermon body. Four things especially should mark every sermon.

1. Unity. A sermon should concentrate on one central idea. This idea should control what he has to say throughout the discussion. Preachers often take close to an hour to speak and say many good things, but the impact of the message is lost because there is no unity in all of the great things said. These are like a shotgun blast whose impact is spread out and soon dissipates its impact. A sermon should be like a rifle shot—singular and to the point.

A sermon with unity has harmony or agreement throughout. A sermon without unity is offensive to taste and lacking in power. Talking which has no controlling idea is not really a sermon. Every division is controlled by the subject and develops it.

To illustrate unity let us take the broad subject of "Faith." Now that subject must be the controlling idea of each division. These could be:

I. The Meaning of Faith

II. The Power of Faith

III. The Demonstration of Faith

This same unity must control the development of each division. For example, the sub-points under "The Power of Faith" (point II) might be:

A. Faith can save (Acts 16:31; Romans 10:10).

B. Faith imparts strength to live the Christian life (Philippians 4:13).

C. Faith can move barriers to service (Matthew 21:21).

When unity is given to the major divisions and then to each minor division, it ensures that unity will be maintained throughout the discourse.

2. *Order.* By order we mean that the divisions of

the sermon are carefully distinguished from one another, and they follow one another in logical sequence. There is a continuity throughout the discussion because of the relationship of each division to the other and to the subject. The material of the sermon should be arranged according to its relative importance. Major divisions should be chosen, and then the minor divisions developed in relation to these.

To use the three divisions discussed under unity and to change the places of I and III would destroy the order in this outline. The mind immediately rejects this order.

    I. The Power of Faith

    II. The Demonstration of Faith

    III. The Meaning of Faith

3. Proportion. Symmetry is balanced proportion. Beauty of form arises from proper proportion. But beauty is not all. A sermon whose divisions fit into the places designed for them in the plan of the sermon is easy to follow and understand. The tendency of preachers generally is to spend too much time on the first point. For this reason they often slide over the development of the following points. For the whole sermon to be developed properly, about the same amount of time should be spent on each one. In fact, your climactic point probably should demand a little extra time. By way of warning, do not climax your sermon in your first point. If you have thirty minutes allotted for a message, a good proportion would be as follows:

Introduction	5 minutes
Point I	7 minutes
Point II	7 minutes
Point III	7 minutes
Conclusion and invitation	4 minutes

4. Progress. A good sermon moves toward a climax. A preacher can make his arrangement as he will, but as the idea is built from one division to the next, the climactic and clinching arguments should be at the end in the application of the message. The preacher should study forms in textbooks, but they are not final. He should develop a form that fits his style of preaching. Some "cornfield" preachers have developed a form that is enviable. They may follow no textbook, but they know how to move to a climax and get their message across.

These four things—unity, order, proportion, and progress—give a message clarity. They also make the message more interesting because the subject is developed well.

B. ADVANTAGES OF A GOOD PLAN

A good plan or arrangement for the body of the sermon has advantages for both the preacher and the people. The advantages for the preacher are:

1. A good plan assists in composing the sermon.

2. A good plan keeps the preacher in line with subject and text.

3. A good plan aids his memory and stimulates his emotional response.

4. A good plan allows consecutive thought, aids emphasis, and makes transition easy.

5. A good plan gives conciseness to the message and gives a better view of the subject as a whole.

6. A good arrangement forms a good habit which makes it easier the next time.

7. A good plan keeps the preacher from forming a bad habit of neglecting or becoming unconcerned about arrangement.

Advantages for the people are:

1. A good plan aids their remembrance of the sermon.

2. A good plan keeps them from wandering (or as one writer put it, from wondering.)

3. A good plan deepens their appreciation for the preacher.

4. A good arrangement makes the sermon easier to be understood and less likely to be misunderstood.

5. Through a well-developed plan, people are more easily persuaded to action.

C. PROCEDURES FOR DEVELOPMENT

A pattern of procedure should be used in the development of each sermon. One preacher described his system in this simple manner: "I tell them what I am going to tell them. I tell them. Then I tell them what I have told them." This is not bad advice. Another writer has suggested three procedures to be used—statement, argument, and illustration. Broadus lists four of these procedures as "functional elements of the sermon." They are explanation, argument, application, and illustration. Day lists them as explanation, confirmation, excitation, and persuasion.

Your goals in preaching are evangelistic, theological, inspirational, ethical, devotional, and incitive. To achieve these goals, these procedures could be summed up in these four terms.

1. Propositions. In a sermon the preacher sets forth certain propositions that he plans to demonstrate. These may not be formally stated, but they dominate his mind as he builds his sermon. They may be in the form of statements or they may be implied by subject and text.

2. Explanations. It is important to define words, to explain the nature of your argument, to make clear what is the exact nature of your propositions. Explanation may take the form of argument. It can be the witness of testimony.

3. Observations. Certain deductions should be made from experience and observation. How something happens, how it works, or how it came about are just some of the observations that need to be made.

4. Illustrations. Illustrations are examples. Every proposition should be amply illustrated in each message. It is in the illustrations that the people are able to see the credibility of your propositions.

81

D. TRANSITION

Transition refers to leaving one division and moving into another. This is sometimes done with difficulty. Perfect transition is made by an expression rather than a phrase. To keep the skeleton of the sermon from being so obvious, avoid such terms as, "And now point four." The last sentence of one division should lead naturally into the first sentence of the next division.

Avoid the formality of using the same words or phrases constantly when passing to another division. This becomes monotonous and even boring to your listeners. Even in one sermon, the same words should not be used. Cultivate a natural variety that comes as naturally to you as variety in your conversation.

Divisions should be apparent throughout though not overly obvious. A person taking notes should be able to detect your major divisions and generally your subdivisions. Opinion is divided as to when to announce divisions formally. Three basic views prevail.

1. Announce your divisions at the beginning. The problem with announcing them at the beginning is that there is a serious loss of anticipation. The congregation can anticipate your movement, and they tend to look for the last point. When the whole sermon is tied closely together and an overview of the whole sermon is needed, go ahead and announce your points.

2. Announce your divisions as you go along. This is probably preferable. As long as you have good transition from one thought to another.

3. Recapitulate at the close of the sermon. This is good and possibly is the most intelligible thing to do. It brings the points all together and focuses attention on your main propositions. To recapitulate is a means of impressing your audience with your main emphases and that impression is probably more lasting than when they are given at the beginning or as you go along.

8

Jllustrations

An illustration is an auxiliary element of the sermon. It has been previously identified as one of the functional elements of the sermon. It is not a distinct part of the sermon as is the introduction or conclusion but may be used as an auxiliary to any of the other distinct parts.

An illustration gives the preacher economy of expression. Just as "one picture is worth a thousand words" so an illustration can save many words. Illustrations, however, should be used sparingly and with discretion. Some so-called sermons are nothing more than a batch of illustrations tied together by a few comments.

A. THE PURPOSE OF ILLUSTRATIONS

The word *illustrate* originally meant "to throw light upon." As a window to a house, so an illustration gives light to a sermon. Someone has said, "Imagination, no less than reason, is God's gift." The use of illustration involves the use of the imagination to bring light to a discourse.

Various writers have used different words to point out the purpose of illustrations. Guthrie used three P's to depict their purpose: proving, painting, and persuading. Macpherson gave a four-fold purpose to illustrations: to clarify, to beautify, to vivify, and to verify. Hoyt says they are for clearness, force, splendor, and memory. Jones says that they are to make truth concrete, interesting, impressive, persuasive, and practical.

To sum up all that these men are saying, consider these four things:

1. *Illustrations arrest attention.* They capture the ear sooner than the general discourse.

2. *Illustrations reveal simply and clearly for better understanding on the part of the hearers.* The clearer, simpler revelation quickens a person's apprehension of the truth.

3. *Illustrations make a more permanent impression.* They are remembered when the rest of the sermon is forgotten. Object lessons are especially good.

4. *Illustrations persuade people to a degree of action that is unattainable by logic alone.* The logic and argument of a preacher may never excite or move to action. But a good illustration promotes a conviction that results in a responsive action.

Preachers should take advantage of the power of illustrations. Some good preachers, possibly those who say the most from a scholar's viewpoint, lose the effect of their message by not giving proper illustration and example. The use of fresh, true-to-life illustration vitalizes a message; however, too many preachers use the same illustrations over and over again. Avoid this.

B. TYPES OF ILLUSTRATIONS

It would be impossible in a brief treatment such as this to list every type of illustration. The purpose here is to remind the preacher of a few possibilities for his use.

1. Biblical. The preacher's chief source of illustration is his Bible. The Bible is not so much a book of formal theology as it is of religious experience. So the preacher should constantly draw on this handbook of the ages, the source of the greatest illustrations of all aspects of religion and theology.

2. Stories. Either true or fictional stories may be used. If they are fictional, be sure that you so designate them. If you are not sure that the story is true, do not tell it as a true story. Another word of advice also is very important. If the incident did not happen to you, do not claim that it did. Some preachers have been guilty of telling certain stories so many times that they come to claim them as personal experiences.

3. Poetic. Poetry makes good illustrations if used properly. It is very expressive and often says in a few words what it would take you many minutes to say.

Avoid long poems. Brief poems or brief excerpts are best.

4. Historical or current events. Both current events and historical events make rich illustrative materials. Many truths can be demonstrated by these.

5. Parables. Jesus used parables often. In fact, He is the recognized master of their use. You might even make up some parables of your own.

6. Object lessons. Brief object lessons can be used which will vividly portray some truth. Do not let the object lesson become the sermon. Make them brief and pointed.

7. Vivid description. Some preachers are very adept with description. Be careful here. Some vivid description of the crucifixion of Christ becomes so gory that it overshadows *who* died. Be dramatic but do not be melodramatic.

8. Flash pictures. The term *flash pictures* is not intended to refer to literal pictures. This is the use of word imagery. A speaker at times can use one word which is so suggestive that it flashes a perfect illustration to the mind of the hearer. Sometimes a phrase or a sentence pithily stated can be very suggestive.

C. SOURCE OF ILLUSTRATIONS

Source books for illustrations are available in bookstores. The problem with these is the fact that a lot of other preachers have the same sources that you have.

Preachers have a bad habit of using the same illustrations that others do and of using them over and over again. The best illustrations are from your own reading, observations, and experiences. Here are some suggested sources of illustrations.

1. The Bible. As mentioned previously Biblical illustrations are those most used by preachers. Never be reluctant about using Bible illustrations. Many good Biblical illustrations are rarely used also.

2. History. History is replete with illustrations. History supplements the Bible as a source of insight into human behavior and needs. History verifies the Biblical account of things. Be a good student of history, and you will not go wanting in illustrative materials.

3. Personal experience. Two special areas of personal experience can be drawn upon. The first is your religious experience. The Bible characters did this. Paul used his conversion experience (Acts 22:6-16; 22:12ff.). Your conversion, your call to the ministry, or some time of special dedication will all make excellent illustrations. The second area is experiences with others with whom you have had intimate contact. Experiences of winning people to Christ or trying to win them to Christ are very good. Experiences drawn from your pastoral ministry may be used as long as you do not give out confidential conversations. Your travels, vacations, and experiences in general afford many illustrations if you will only be observant.

4. Science. A preacher should not be completely ignorant in the area of science. Occasional reading to keep abreast of advances in science will enrich your source of illustration.

5. Biography. Both biography and autobiography afford a wealth of materials. Of course, it is from the lives of great Christian men and women that we may glean the most.

6. Poetry. Read poetry for your own benefit and in a search for material to illustrate.

7. Drama. Shakespeare and other great dramatists give some deep insights into human nature.

8. Fiction. Be careful here. Do not go overboard. But a preacher should occasionally read fiction for personal enjoyment as well as for illustration.

9. Your own creations. If you make up a story, parable, or illustration of any kind, be sure that you do not give the impression that it actually happened to you.

D. THINGS TO BE AVOIDED

Illustrations can be misused or overused. Here are several common mistakes that should be avoided.

1. The use of illustrations as decorations. Illustrations should never be used purely as ornament or adornment. Trying to make the sermon beautiful without the aim of trying to get the message across is not a legitimate use of illustration.

2. Building the sermon around illustrations. Some sermons give the impression that text and subject were chosen for the illustrations rather than the illustrations being chosen to illustrate truths found in the text and subject.

3. *The use of illustrations that have to be illustrated.* If an illustration is so deep that it has to be explained, it will not serve its purpose. Such an illustration would confuse rather than give light.

4. *Illustrating the obvious.* This is the opposite of the previous mistake. Some things are clear and need no illustration. Leave them alone.

5. *The use of illustration for a show or display for self-glory.* Remember it is truth not self which you are presenting.

6. *The use of sameness in kind of illustration.* Any repetitious pattern in your preaching is to be avoided. To constantly use the same type of illustration will make your preaching monotonous.

7. *Taking for granted that people know Bible illustrations.* They do not generally. Do not be satisfied to illustrate something by saying, "You remember how David loved Jonathan." That is not enough. Tell them.

E. PRESERVING ILLUSTRATIONS

The big task is having illustrations available when you need them. Your experiences and reading are replete with illustrations every day. When you need them, they may not be so handy. Here are some suggestions for preserving illustrations and having them at hand when you need them.

1. Mark your books and magazines and keep file cards on them. Cards may be filed by subject or by Scripture passage. Already printed cards are available at bookstores selling Christian literature.

2. Keep notebooks on your observations. An observation may be made today, forgotten tomorrow, and needed the next day. Coming out of New Orleans across Lake Ponchartrain on an especially tempestuous day, this writer viewed that mighty lake in turmoil and was reminded of Isaiah 57:20: "The wicked are like the troubled sea." Such an experience stored away can be useful if that verse is ever used as a text.

3. Use an envelope system for filing papers and clippings. Envelopes can be arranged also according to subjects or according to Scripture divisions.

4. Develop a scrapbook for short articles, poems, quotations, or other materials that would fit in it. Small file cards might serve the same function if articles can be pasted on cards for filing.

File cabinets can be used for the envelopes. Some materials can be kept in folders if care is taken to keep it from just becoming a mass of material. The important thing is: KEEP UP WITH YOUR ILLUSTRATIONS.

9
The Conclusion

"The conclusion of the sermon is that part by which the central thought in the main body is practically applied," wrote Fisk. Although some application should be involved throughout the sermon, it is in the conclusion that the most forceful application is made. Napoleon is quoted as saying, "I reserve my heaviest battalions for the close." What is true in warfare makes sense also in preaching. Your most forceful application should come in the conclusion.

A. THE IMPORTANCE OF THE CONCLUSION

To close weakly is to impair the effect of the whole sermon. So the conclusion is a vital part of the sermon.

1. The completeness of a sermon depends on it. A lecture may close with a description of some subject. A simple talk may close when the subject has been covered. But a sermon is not complete without an application of what has been presented. Like a house with no exit or an interstate highway with no off ramp, so is a sermon with no conclusion.

2. The effectiveness of a sermon depends on it. To present truth and then to make no application to the hearers is to leave them dangling. It is in the conclusion that you call the hearers to give an account of their responsibility to the truth presented.

3. The moment of decision is near and much depends upon it. Preachers often count decisions by the number who respond at the altar service. In reality every person present makes some type of decision. The conclusion should be effectively presented to elicit the proper decision from each hearer.

The importance of the conclusion is suggested in the Scriptures. There prophets and apostles alike stated the applications of their messages. So did our Lord. When a message comes from God, it is one to be applied to lives and demands a decision from its hearers.

B. MARKS OF A GOOD CONCLUSION

Since the conclusion is so vital to a message, it is important that it meet certain standards.

1. Well prepared. John Knight said, "The only part of my speech that I prepare is the conclusion. I always know *how* and *when* I'm going to stop." Preachers often omit any preparation for their conclusions. Their weak finish is evidence of this. Preachers should make a habit of writing out a part of their conclusions. This will help them in making the best choice of words.

2. *Natural and appropriate.* Your closing of the main body of the sermon should lead naturally into your conclusion. "Finally" and "and now in conclusion" should not always be in the introductory words to your conclusion. The conclusion should be appropriate for the sermon, because it is directly related to the sermon. The central thought of the main body is that which must be applied in the conclusion. To be natural and appropriate it will complete the sermon as it should.

3. *Clear.* Clarity is one mark which is absolutely necessary in a good conclusion. You have finished the sermon, how now can it be applied? Be sure that your hearers know exactly how it is to be applied to them. Make sure it is "conclusion and not confusion."

4. *Short.* Many preachers leave the impression they do not know how to close. They roam here and there. They make you want to cry out, "Quit now. You're through." The wise preacher will cultivate conciseness in his conclusion. Clinch your message with a short, pithy application.

5. *Single.* You have one vital issue at stake in your message. Drive that issue home to the minds of your hearers. You may contrast this issue with another in your conclusion, but do not lose the force of the issue by bringing in other issues.

6. *Persuasive.* Your desire in preaching is, by the help of God, to make a difference in human lives. You

want to elicit some new vow, to release a soul from the bondage of sin, to bring surrender of some new area of a Christian's life, or to cause someone to more resolutely bear the believer's cross. Your conclusion is the place to nail down that response.

7. *Personal.* The purpose of the conclusion is to cause the hearer to say, "This means me." Each one to whom the message is directed should cry out, "Lord, what wilt thou have me to do?" (Acts 9:6). Do not let your sermon die out and be wasted. Close like Nathan to David with "Thou art the man" (2 Samuel 12:7). Use the note of direct personal appeal always.

C. TYPES OF CONCLUSIONS

Conclusions will vary with the different types of sermons. Even in the same type of sermons, the preacher should have variety in his conclusions. A few suggestions follow.

1. *Recapitulation.* This does not mean to repeat your sermon. Preachers are sometimes guilty of this. It means that you repeat (briefly and possibly in different words) enough to revive the recollection of what has been said. This can be used very forcefully to bring home the full impact of your sermon.

2. *Practical application.* To make a practical application to his audience, the preacher must have a warm religious experience of his own. He must apply his message in intense earnestness. What is not his experience cannot become that of his hearers. Every message

needs to be practically applied in some way; although, this will not be the major emphasis in each conclusion.

3. Contrasting truth. Jesus' conclusion to the Sermon on the Mount is a good illustration of contrasting truths. There He gave the contrast between the rock and sand foundations.

4. Warning. If evils have been preached against, warning of some nature would be fitting in the conclusion. For the wavering this warning might take the form of admonition. To the weak it could well take the form of encouragement or simple exhortation.

5. Earnest appeal. The message at times will demand an earnest appeal. On occasion that strong appeal will be to the intellect. There will be other times that the preacher must appeal to the will of man to act. There are times to appeal to the deep emotions of man. This should not be overplayed.

6. Poetic. Poetry is good. Take these two words of advice, however. Use only short excerpts from poems. Do not use poetry too often in closing.

7. Illustration. Use this cautiously also. Illustrations take time. For an illustration to fittingly close the sermon, it must be specifically related to the main emphasis of the sermon.

8. Final sentence. This can be impressive. William Carey closed a message with this great thought: "Wherefore, let us undertake great things for God and expect great things from Him." Alexander Whyte built a sermon up to a very climactic point and closed with this cry: "Now let it work!" It is said that the spiritual effect was overwhelming.

D. CONCLUSIONS TO AVOID

There are many other types of conclusions that are desirable, but there are several which should be avoided. Among them are these.

1. The humorous. A message of the gospel should not close on a humorous note. Humor has its place in preaching, but the conclusion is surely not that place. A humorous note at the close will destroy the serious intent of the message.

2. The boisterous. Whirlwind, tempest, and thunder have their places in sermons; but such should be the exception rather than the rule in the conclusion. A more quiet and measured close following the surge and passion of a mighty sermon can have great effect.

3. The tired out. A quiet close should never give the impression of being fatigued or run-down. Quiet oratory in a conclusion does not mean that passion and feelings played out. It merely means that the dramatic tension has been relaxed so that appeal can be made to the quietness of the inner man.

4. A new idea. Nothing unrelated should be introduced in the conclusion. A new idea at this point tends to confuse any hearer. It is distracting to the train of thought which has been followed throughout the sermon.

5. *A common pattern.* Never let the congregation guess what is to come "in closing." When every sermon closes in the same manner, the tendency is for each message to lose its effect. Remember that the repetition of any pattern in preaching is monotonous for your listeners.

As closing suggestions, in your conclusion, always (1) master your conclusion, (2) close hopefully, and (3) lean hard on authority for what you say.

E. THE INVITATION

Rather than discussing the invitation as a separate chapter, a word will be added here in regard to it. Oddly enough, books on homiletics have very little to say, if anything, about the invitation. This is probably because of the fact that many of today's preachers do not give an invitation for their hearers to respond and make an open decision in regard to the message presented.

This is exactly what an invitation is. After the preacher has preached his sermon, the invitation is the opportunity for the hearers of the Word to make public their response to the message. To a message on salvation, the invitation is to be saved. A message on backsliding allows an invitation for the backslider to return to the Lord. A message on some great gospel truth should be followed by an invitation to Christians to give assent to that truth.

The public invitation is the most important part of

the worship service. Souls are lost and church growth is stunted by ineffective invitations. Poor planning for harvest results in lost crops for farmers. Salesmen fail to sell their products when they do not know how to close the sale. So preachers who give an ineffective invitation fail to draw in souls.

Two theories prevail about the relationship of the invitation to the conclusion. Some would view the invitation as a part of the conclusion. Others would say that the invitation is a distinct part of the sermon just as the conclusion is. Whether it is blended with the conclusion or separated from it, the preacher needs to make invitation a vital part of his preaching.

One bad practice is the giving of an invitation to come to the altar after every sermon. Invitations for salvation should always be by an invitation to the altar or to a counsel room. However, not all sermons close with an invitation to the unsaved. Some sermons should close with the invitation for believers to go forth and put into action the principle challenge of the message. Other invitations could be to raise one's hand as an indication of response to a challenge. The invitation should not conflict with the main import of the message. An invitation to salvation would be out of place following a message on tithing. However, if a lost person responded because he was touched, no one would gainsay his decision.

There are four basic types of invitation: (1) to the unsaved, (2) to the backslider, (3) for special service such as to the ministry, to the mission field, or to other special service, and (4) to a particular challenge of the gospel such as clean living, tithing, or a closer walk.

Make each invitation clear and specific. There should be no doubt in the minds of the hearers as to who is included in the invitation or who is expected to respond.

Tell them specifically what to do. If they are to raise their hands, indicate that they are to do so. If the invitation is for sinners to come to the altar, give them specific instructions and let them know what to expect. Remember that a sinner is not accustomed to being at the front of the church and standing before an audience. Let them know that someone will meet them at the altar and will tell them exactly what to do.

After the invitation is spoken, the time for response is usually accompanied by music. This is good but is not essential. The quietness of a moment of silence may be all that is necessary. Generally speaking the preacher should not leave the pulpit until the invitation is completed. Trained workers should meet the penitents at the altar and deal with them.

10
Preparation of a Sermon

The preparation of a sermon is not something to be done on Saturday night before it is to be preached on Sunday. For a preacher who has weekly speaking engagements, it is an involved task for the week. It is a blessed thing when a preacher makes preaching his chief vocation in life. That was the aim of the early apostles in Jerusalem. They chose associates to minister about the other things while they gave themselves "continually to prayer, and to the ministry of the word" (Acts 6:4).

Sermon preparation begins with the preparation of the preacher. He should begin, continue, and end his preparation with prayer. Every sermon should be saturated with prayer and communion with God. The preacher should always be filled with a strong desire to help his people. That desire will prompt him to intense preparation to meet their need. At the same time the preacher would have a strong determination to please God. What is God's message? What do I say as His representative? These are questions that should dominate his hours of preparation.

A. METHOD OF PROCEDURE

In ᴛhe actual preparation of the sermon each preacher should develop a method of procedure which he follows. That procedure should not be to read someone else's sermon and use his outline. Find a method of procedure that is suitable to you and follow it each week.

Ilion T. Jones suggests the following procedure: (1) Get the mind started. (2) Browse and brood. (3) Make a tentative outline. (4) Write out the sermon. (5) Give the sermon a final checking. (6) Prepare yourself for preaching it. Henry Sloane Coffin used the following method: (1) Decide upon a pressing need of the congregation. (2) Select the aspect of the gospel which meets that need. (3) Look for a text that embodies that message. (4) Study the text for its full meaning. (5) Make an outline with a few notes and suggestions for illustrations. (6) Write it out whether it is to be read or delivered extemporaneously. (7) Correct and polish it.

Sermons will sometimes come to one's mind from the reading of the Scriptures. Others will arise from some need which he observes among his flock. For this reason let this writer suggest this procedure:

1. Keep the mind alert for a text or subject which the Holy Spirit impresses upon your mind.

2. If the text is first impressed, seek now for a subject; if the subject came first, seek now for a text which embodies that message.

3. Research the text fully that you may become

full of its meaning.

4. Develop an outline and select illustrations for appropriate points.

5. Write out an occasional sermon for your own benefit.

6. Correct and perfect the sermon in your final study hour before it is to be preached.

B. OUTLINING A SERMON

In essence every preacher has some type of an outline. It may be a poor one. It may consist of nothing more than three scraps of paper marking three Scriptures to which he plans to make reference. But he should do more than this. The Holy Spirit can lead a person just as surely in outlining a message in his study (in fact, more so) as he can in purely extemporaneous address after he gets into the pulpit. Now this does not mean that a preacher has to take his outline notes to the pulpit. Some preachers memorize the outline so that their message appears to be purely extemporaneous. This is good.

There are several advantages to the preacher in outlining. Among them are: (1) It aids him in the development of his thought. (2) It keeps the preacher on track. (3) It assists him in keeping proportion in the various parts of the sermon. (4) It assures movement of thought in the sermon.

There are also several advantages to the people

which should not be overlooked: (1) An outline enables the hearers to understand what is being said and to see where the preacher is headed. (2) An outline prevents misunderstanding. (3) An outline provides the hearers with a needed emotional rhythm. (4) An outline is a great aid to remembrance.

An outline does not just happen. It results from intense study and labor. The mind works somewhat like a computer. A computer can only feed out what has been fed into it. So can the mind. Until the mind is saturated with the Word and related facts, it cannot produce an organized outline for a message. However, when it is full of its subject, the mind has logical powers that organize and produce intelligible thought patterns. Therefore, the preacher should not try outlining on the first day he is impressed with a text or subject. The outlining should begin only after a process of study.

C. WRITING SERMONS

Every preacher should occasionally write out a sermon. Not only will it develop certain possibilities within him, but it will allow him to preserve his message for posterity. The ministries of men like T. DeWitt Talmadge and Charles Spurgeon have been perpetuated and multiplied because of their sermons which were written and put in print. The preaching of most preachers ceases at their death because they have written nothing.

There are certainly some disadvantages to writing. Writing consumes a lot of the minister's time. A sermon to be effective in writing must have much more care and effort than a spoken one. Writing can make a person dependent upon this practice. The time may come that he will not have time to follow this procedure. Another disadvantage lies in the fact that though it may make the preacher cover his materials more completely, it does not ensure that it will always be done more thoroughly. A poorly written sermon will be a blessing to no one.

There are certain advantages, however, in the writing of sermons. The preacher should consider these:

1. The practice of writing will develop one's facility in writing. Practice may not "make perfect," but it surely will improve one's abilities in this area.

2. Writing makes it easier for the preacher to fix his mind on his subject. It pinpoints the task before him and does not allow him to leave it so easily.

3. Writing compels the preacher to greater completeness of preparation. When you read your thoughts on paper, they appear much more shallow than when verbalized. Seeing this, the preacher will work harder to have something to say and to say it in a better way.

4. This better and more complete preparation will result in greater excellence of style. This improvement will overflow into the preacher's oral delivery also. It will add quality to the content and delivery of the sermon.

5. And as previously suggested, writing will allow

the sermon to be used on a subsequent occasion such as for publication. Many religious magazines are glad to get good sermons for publication. The preacher may want to publish a volume of his own sermons some day.

One clergyman was said to have boasted to another, "When I go up to the pulpit, I never know the subject of my sermon." Another preacher replied, "No, and I understand your congregation doesn't when you come down." Preacher, preparation is as much a part of your preaching as delivery. Take this word of advice and prepare every message well.

11

The Delivery of a Sermon

The proper delivery of a message received from God should be the constant burden of the preacher's heart. It is not enough to have a message from God; he must effectively speak that message to others. He is not just to speak words or beat the air when he stands behind the pulpit; he is to convey the truth of God to the awaiting audience.

The preacher's aim is to use every capacity of his personality to convey his message as clearly and as persuasively as possible. No talent, no energy, and no ability of his is to be neglected as he seeks to lead his hearers to a deep awareness of his message from God. He aspires to bring their thought, feeling, and life into accord with God's will as expressed by his message. If such a sense does not come to possess the preacher, his motives and aim in preaching are too low.

A. REQUISITES TO EFFECTIVE DELIVERY

For a preacher to achieve such an effect through

his preaching as that mentioned above, certain requisites must be met by him. Effective preaching is not an automatic result of having a card of ministerial standing in your pocket. Here are some factors that will contribute to effective preaching.

1. Have something to say worth saying. When you approach the pulpit, do so with the sense that "I have a message from God which you must hear." If two hundred people are gathered for the preaching hour to hear you, make sure that you do not waste two hundred hours of God-given time. Time is valuable. Only a message from God is worth this amount of time.

2. Have your treatment well arranged. For your message to be most fully effective, it should be well prepared beforehand.

3. Be thoroughly familiar with what you propose to say. Always know more about your text and subject than you plan to say. Good water comes from deep wells of water. Good sermons arise out of a depth of knowledge and experience.

4. Spend some time thinking over and praying about your message right before the time to speak. Be newly warmed by its effect before you try to speak it to your people. The effect of the message upon the people will be measured in direct proportion to its effect upon you.

5. Arrange your activities so as to be in good physical condition. Saturday night suppers and late hours on the night before you preach can diminish your ability to think and to deliver your message effectively.

Avoid such things when possible.

6. Be yourself. This is false advice in one sense. We labor to improve upon self and to develop self. It means to be yourself in that you are relaxed and do not put on airs. Be casual. Do not be artificial in your delivery.

B. METHODS OF DELIVERY

The three basic modes of delivery are reading, recitation, and extemporaneous address. Reading as a method has not been popular for many years. However, some of the world's most famous sermons were read. It is said that Jonathan Edwards' famous sermon, "Sinners in the Hands of an Angry God," was read by the near-sighted Edwards by dim candlelight. Its effect was overpowering. But reading of sermons is not popular in today's evangelical churches.

Recitation is speaking a memorized sermon. This, like read sermons, is not popular either. Preachers probably shy away from this because of the work involved. Men with great minds like R. G. Lee in essence knew their sermons from memory as they approached the pulpit.

Extemporaneous address is the most popular and most widely used method of delivery used in preaching in conservative, evangelistic churches. This term is not usually used to infer impromptu preaching with no advance preparation. A better term might be "free preaching." This term would describe a carefully prepared message delivered as extemporaneous preaching without a manuscript. Notes may or may not be used in free preaching.

In free preaching there will always be some preparation. The subject and text have been mastered. Sometimes even words and phrases have been mastered. Above all, the heart has been thoroughly prepared for the sermon.

Here is a list of advantages to be found in extemporaneous address:

1. *It is the popular method.* Extemporaneous speech avoids the objections to the other methods.

2. *It gives competence in speech without immediate preparation.* It is much more convenient than having to prepare a manuscript for reading or recitation. It allows the preacher to "be instant in season, out of season."

3. *It is the natural way of speaking and allows the speaker to rise to the best delivery of which he is capable.* Extemporaneous preaching has been called "the crown and radiance of all eloquence." It does the most complete justice to the task of preaching of any method.

4. *It allows the speaker to alter forms of expression or his manner of delivery to suit his own feeling or the response of his hearers.* This allows this type of address to combine the largest number of excellencies. New ideas may be inserted as they rise to his mind. It allows him to adapt words or style to the need of the moment.

5. *It allows time for general improvement and*

other pastoral work. An average preacher who wrote or memorized two or three sermons a week would have time for nothing else.

6. It trains the preacher to think more rapidly and to depend less on external helps. Thus it gives him a freedom unknown by the other methods.

Although extemporaneous preaching is recommended to every preacher, there are some words of counsel that should be heeded. Here are some suggestions: (1) Do not adopt this method just because you think it is the easiest. (2) Keep your mind well-stocked and trained to accuracy in the recall of facts and illustrations and especially of the Scriptures. (3) Although you may not be writing and memorizing, constantly practice composition and correct grammar. (4) Do not neglect the careful preparation of your sermon plan. (5) Discipline yourself in composure. There will be times that will "rattle" you. (6) Always prepare yourself mentally and have your outline in hand or strong in your mind.

C. THE PREACHER'S VOICE

The preacher's greatest tool is his voice. He only has one. It cannot be replaced. He should take good care of it so that it will last for a lifetime. This writer heard one preacher preach who was past ninety. His voice was as clear as a bell. He had taken good care of it.

The preacher should spend some time in study of

voice and speech. As an example, he should know the powers of the voice: compass, volume, penetration, and melody. *Compass* is the range of pitch in the voice. This range can be improved by singing. *Volume*, of course, is the quantity of sound which a voice can produce. Volume can be improved by physical exercise and habitual, proper carriage of the body. *Penetration* is the distance to which one can be heard. A voice with volume alone may not carry too far. It needs also the quality of penetration. This can be improved by vocal exercises such as the utterance of vowel sounds and the articulation of the consonants. *Melody* is sweetness and flexibility of voice. This is a desirable trait which can be improved by singing and keeping the organs of speech in a healthy condition.

Good speech is a means of getting your message across to the audience. Good speech comes from: (1) *Good breathing.* There must be an adequate amount of air passing without tension across your vocal chords. (2) *Good tone production.* This brings pleasantness of voice. The preacher needs to develop musical, clear, flexible tones of adequate range and in volume suitable to the occasion. (3) *Good resonance.* This is sound production which results from a balanced use of the resonators in a manner suitable for the occasion. It involves the amplification of certain tones. (4) *Good articulation.* This is word production or enunciation. A coordinated use of the speech organs produces this. Proper enunciation results when one speaks his words and syllables distinctly.

There are several ways to improve the voice including those already mentioned. Here are five basic suggestions.

1. Form and maintain good habits of speech.

2. Cultivate good general health through proper exercise and other health measures.

3. Join heartily in the singing with the congregation.

4. Read aloud for voice practice.

5. Practice the proper management of the voice even in ordinary conversation.

The proper management of the voice when you are preaching is vital for the care of your voice and for the proper delivery of your message. There are several rules suggested by Broadus which should be followed. Follow these especially: (1) Do not begin on too high a key. This leads to shrillness. (2) Do not let the voice drop on the last words of the sentence. This is the source of one of the most monotonous habits among preachers. (3) Take a breath before your lungs are completely exhausted and generally keep them well filled. This avoids the "hillbilly whang" or "preacher's bark" that is considered a mark of real preaching among some groups. (4) See that the remotest hearers can hear you. Preach to the back row or to the balcony. (5) Use variety of pitch, force, and speed. Exercise all your powers of speech for best effect. (6) Do not keep your mind on your voice. Develop good natural habits of speech. Preoccupation with your voice will result in tenseness which can be detrimental to it.

D. THE PREACHER'S STYLE

A preacher's style is his characteristic manner of expressing himself. Just as each person has his own handwriting, so each preacher has a manner of expressing himself through his preaching. Someone has said, "The style is the man." This is so true. But what is man's style naturally may not be good. Each man's style may be disciplined and improved without his losing his individuality.

The tendency is to develop faulty styles. Some preachers develop a flowery style that is highly ornamental or a spacious style that has grandeur as its goal. The preacher is full of impressive tone and expanded statement. The polished style developed by others is conspicuous for being overly well tailored and well kempt. The preacher with the fine style uses words and phrases for their own sake. Then there is the opposite of all these. Some preachers develop a simple style. It is marked by an effort to be common and non-homiletical. Often poor English is practiced to show how common one can be.

In reality an effective style is marked by simple words, few words, and expressive words. You achieve style by two simple things—study and practice. Three suggestions have been made by Broadus as a means to improving style: (1) *Study language.* Your voice is your tool. Language is the vehicle of expression. No one ever achieves complete facility in the use of his native tongue. Studying language should be a lifelong work of the preacher. Even the study of foreign languages will make one more efficient in his own tongue. (2) *Study literature.* When you study good literature, you are a pupil of men and women who know how to express themselves. This is something that you want to achieve. (3) *Careful practice in writing and speaking.* This has already been suggested in previous statements but cannot be overemphasized. Practice with care so that the faulty will be corrected and the good will be strengthened. A practice of good speaking confirms one in a good style.

Broadus also lists four qualities that should characterize good style. These are:

1. Clearness. This is simplicity of thought. The masters of the pulpit have never used big words and hard to understand phrases.

2. Energy. Energy is animation, force, or passion in the speaker. A preacher needs an energetic nature, vigorous thinking, an earnest, passionate feeling, and a resolute purpose.

3. Elegance. Elegance is not ornamental speech. It refers to a quality of speech. Though subordinate to energy and clearness, elegance in style is to be desired.

4. Imagination. Imagination as a quality of style refers to thinking by seeing in contrast to reasoning. A preacher needs to be creative in his thinking. Imagination allows the preacher to bring facts from his memory and to set them in new relationships.

Some elements of a preacher's style are natural gifts. Other elements must be acquired. Blessed is the preacher who improves his style so that his preaching is effective.

D. ASPECTS OF ACTION

Action is the speech of the body. It is natural for any person speaking even in normal conversation. It is something very desirable in a preacher and can add to the effectiveness of his delivery. Action may range in a preacher from the antics of Billy Sunday who climbed on the pulpit and broke chairs to the quiet preacher whose main action is the expression of his countenance.

The expression of the countenance is a part of action. The countenance of the face usually assumes an expression appropriate to the preacher's attitude toward his message. The expression of the countenance should be natural and unplanned. Speakers sometime form bad habits through a false smile or even a false show of seriousness.

Gestures are a vital part of the action of the body. Students of homiletics were once taught how to gesture. The tendency in recent years has been to encourage gestures only as the preacher is naturally prompted to do. Gestures involve the movement of the whole person. Cicero was said to have had eloquence in the tips of his fingers. Blaikie said that one speaker could produce a magic effect by moving his elbows. It is not natural for a

116

preacher to stand still. But whether it is the movement of his hands, his head, or his whole body, the gesture should be appropriate to the effect one hopes to gain.

The posture of the preacher is a part of action. He should arrange his body in the pulpit so that he will be allowed to function in the most efficient manner. However, the arrangement of his body in the pulpit should not be so awkward as to call attention to itself.

A preacher should avoid any movement or gesture that becomes monotonous. Some sway back and forth in the pulpit. Some wave their hands up and down. Some put their hands together before them and repeatedly gesture with the two hands clasped. Such gestures are distracting to the listeners and add nothing to the message.

Excessive action can be very disconcerting to the audience. This writer watched one preacher who was never still. He ran from side to side, around the pulpit, and down to the front pew and back. It was tiring just to watch him.

The timing of each gesture is very important. Generally a gesture should slightly precede the word or phrase it is intended to emphasize. If it is simultaneous or follows, it tends to lose its power.

A preacher's gestures should be suggestive only. If a reference to the heavens is made, the preacher should not point to the heavens and look that way. He should merely make a slight gesture upward while maintaining his eye contact with the audience.

D. FREEDOM IN DELIVERY

Every preacher aspires to freedom in delivery. Of course, the fulness of freedom can only come as the Holy Spirit overshadows him as he speaks. That too will only come as the preacher has done his part. Full and careful preparation will lead to free delivery. His resolve to speak well, regular habits of study and work, proper attention to his health, and pulpit experience itself will lead to freedom.

If the preacher properly prepares and trains himself for delivery of his message, these things will result:

1. His powers and abilities will be used forcefully in achieving his aim.

2. His style will be pleasing and make the sermon more attractive to his hearers.

3. Self-consciousness will be prevented.

4. A ministerial tone will be avoided.

5. His powers of expression will be fully utilized.

6. The impression he makes will be powerful because he controls his emphasis.

7. The preacher will be the master of each occasion on which he fills the sacred stand.

8. Because he will be the master of the situation, he will be inspired for preaching with confidence.

Are you called to be a preacher? If so, God demands nothing less than your best. The condition of lost man demands your best. Surely your own self-respect cries out for you to give your best effort to be the most forceful preacher possible.

9 780892 650187